I0125974

Francis Francis

Fish-Culture

A Practical Guide to the Modern System of Breeding and Rearing Fish

Francis Francis

Fish-Culture
A Practical Guide to the Modern System of Breeding and Rearing Fish

ISBN/EAN: 9783337139421

Printed in Europe, USA, Canada, Australia, Japan

Cover: Foto ©Andreas Hilbeck / pixelio.de

More available books at **www.hansebooks.com**

See pages 58, 59, and 63.

FISH·CULTURE:

A PRACTICAL GUIDE

TO THE

MODERN SYSTEM OF BREEDING AND REARING FISH.

BY

FRANCIS FRANCIS.

WITH NUMEROUS ILLUSTRATIONS.

LONDON:

ROUTLEDGE, WARNE, AND ROUTLEDGE,

2, FARRINGDON STREET.

NEW YORK: 56, WALKER STREET.

1863.

LONDON :
E. CLAY, SON, AND TAYLOR, PRINTERS,
BREAD STREET HILL.

PREFACE.

THE practice of Pisciculture has become a matter of such public interest and importance, that I am induced to put forth this little treatise, not because no works on the subject have been published before, but because there are many points which are extremely interesting in the science, and which, in all probability, will become the most popular part of it, which have been hitherto almost overlooked.

My design is not only to show my readers how they may hatch the eggs of fish, but how they can best bestow their energies, and direct their studies and experiments, as a means towards increasing the supply of wholesome fish food ; to review the various fresh-water fish found in Great Britain, and point out those which are most valuable to us, and how they may best be distributed, cultivated, and increased ; and

further, to consider the merits of such fish as
it may be advisable to acclimatize, but which
are not at present included in our Fauna. Com-
prehensively considered, my plan is to indicate
how water may be made most productive, and
what should be done with those vast aqueous
deserts of lake and stream which are now comparatively valueless, but which would be mines
of wealth to us were it not for the ignorance
which generally pertains to everything vitally
connected with this subject.

I do not pretend myself to write upon this
matter as a master, but rather as a student
yet on the threshold, hoping to engage others
in the investigation of that which may be called
a new science, and which any one may engage
themselves in who can command the simple
accessory of a bowl of water;—a science, the
workings and effects of which have to be discovered, and in which there are honours and
profitable fame to be won ; while vast benefits to
the human race in general, and our own country
in particular, will flow from an extended knowledge of it. I have glimpses—afar off it may
be—of the valuable life which should and may

teem in every pool of water and running brook, if this science I point to were brought out as it should be. I believe water—neglected, ill-used water—if properly applied, to be much more valuable than land, through its greater productive powers; [1] and where the best species of fish, as salmon and trout, can be cultivated, capable of yielding a revenue very far exceeding that of land.

Water requires few or none of those expenses demanded on land. Left to itself, it produces and reproduces to a degree which, computing by acreage, very far transcends the land. What would our rivers and streams be worth if brought back only to a state of nature, if man had not (instead of cultivating them) almost destroyed them? But ought we to be satisfied to restore our streams to their natural state, and content to leave them so? Is water-culture so

[1] What edible animal is there that exists on land, which possesses the capability of reproducing 9,000 of its own size in a period little exceeding eighteen months? This can, however, be performed by a grilse of eight or nine pounds' weight. A grilse of this size will deposit, say, 9,000 ova in about fifteen or sixteen months; the fry from this ova go down to the sea, and in two or three months more they have been known to come back to the river as grilse of from five to ten pounds' weight.

difficult a study, so recondite in its secrets, so
partial and uncertain in its results, that it should
not vie, by the means of study and experiment,
with agriculture?   Surely the small results
already obtained do not tell us so; much rather
do they encourage us to pursue our inquiries,
that we may win from Nature her secrets and
profit thereby.   We know something of the
science, but the main secrets remain to be
explored.

People are apt to consider the hatching of fish-
ova a very difficult, astonishing, and precarious
operation.   It is natural that they should do so,
as the process is new to them.   But there is
no real difficulty in the matter; any one can
compass it.   The appliances are of the simplest
kind.   Indeed, I would undertake to hatch a
hundred young salmon with the aid of a cheese-
plate and a tumbler of water.   But the point
chiefly to be considered is, how are fish to be
fed and fattened when they are hatched; what
suits them, and what does not?   We often
hear of the fish in certain waters dying off
without being able to discover the cause.   Some
weed, or insect, or other matter which is very

prejudicial to fish, may have become mixed
with the water; and we ought to be able to
detect the cause at once, and with certainty.
We ought to know how such things are to be
prevented, and what the diseases of fish spring
from. But do we?

The agriculturist knows to a head or two
what amount of stock his farm will carry. He
knows what kinds of roots are best suited,
not only for stock to feed on, but for his
various fields to grow. The cold land suits
one thing—the dry land another. This will
grow swedes and that corn, this grass or what
not. He knows what species of food, and what
variety of it, will fatten his stock the quickest.
He knows what roots and cereals are the most
productive and pay best, and in what order they
should be planted. He knows what breeds of
stock suit his farm, and where to put them, and
when it is most profitable to him to get rid of
them. He would never think of putting a
Southdown sheep on a Highland sheepwalk,
nor a Welsh runt on a Hereford pasture, &c.
As a breeder and feeder, he knows how to cross-
breed and feed his stock, so as even to change

the very frames and carcasses of his cattle into
the shape most favourable to his interests ; and
how has he arrived at all this, but by study and
experiment ?

Contrast our knowledge of water-culture with
that of agriculture, and the result is simply
degrading.   We should know what kind of
food suits our various fish best, and what conditions best produce that food, and how those
conditions are best to be cultivated, *so that such
food may be self-producing.*   Hence it will be seen
that the habits of all the insects and plants found
in water, and their correlative agreements and
dependence upon each other, must be studied.
Going lower still, the conditions that suit these
conditions, even to their chemical and microsco-
pical analysis, peep out, and a grand scheme of
a new science, a new phase of creation, is, as I
have said, dimly foreshadowed, in which the food
of man is the dependent consideration.

Were we to study to understand the position
in creation which every insect fills, the great
secret would not be to us the jumble which it
is, and we should begin to appreciate the beauty

and harmony of the works of the Creator, and
to see the wickedness and absurdity of interfering
to disarrange them. The aquarium has hitherto
been an interesting scientific trifle; henceforth
it should be a link in this great chain of obser-
vation. It will be seen, by the few remarks I
have made, that this science requires to be, and
is capable of being, widely popularized. I shall
touch further on these matters in the body of
my work as I find occasion.

It may be urged that, in the succeeding pages,
I have taken somewhat too wide a range of subjects into the study of Pisciculture. I cannot
think so, however, if this science is to become
as popular among us and as beneficial to us as
it should be. The mere hatching and rearing of
small fish appears to me to be but an integral
part of Pisciculture; and it will not be denied
that considerations as to the best kinds of fish
to encourage, and how to encourage them, with
the best methods of producing suitable food for
them, are necessarily points of as much importance as that of bringing them into the world.

CONTENTS.

INTRODUCTORY CHAPTER.

CHAPTER I.

CHAPTER II.

CHAPTER III.

CHAPTER IX.

CHAPTER XI.

APPENDIX.

FISH CULTURE.

INTRODUCTORY CHAPTER.

THE ORIGIN AND PROGRESS OF PISCICULTURE.

PISCICULTURE is said to have been originally discovered by the Chinese, those barbarians to whom
civilization owes so large a debt, even for its silk and
its tea, and many most ingenious and useful inven-
tions. The art was practised by the Chinese from
time immemorial, and the scale upon which they
have employed it is far larger, and more comprehen-
sive, than has been since adopted. Planting in
suitable places in their rivers large posts, to which
a framework was attached, they placed thereon
faggots and hurdles for the fish to spawn on. That
operation completed, they removed the hurdles, &c.,
collected the eggs, and either hatched them under
their own immediate supervision, or stocked other
streams with them. By this simple but effective

B

process, the rivers of China have come to abound with fish, to such an extent, that it forms the staple of food amongst the lower classes.

The Romans followed the Chinese in their practice of pisciculture. During the republic, the art was employed to supply the wants of the nation; under the empire it was extended and improved by the luxurious nobles, until it became a hobby upon which the ambitious gourmand lavished his treasure to an extent which, even in the present age, would be regarded with wonder. Speaking of the achievements of Lucullus, M. Jourdier (one of the French piscicul-turists, who has written an interesting work upon the culture of fish, leeches, &c. &c.), quoting M. Guezon Duval, says that, "at his house at Tusculum, on the borders of the Gulf of Naples, he dug large trenches, or canals, running from his fishponds to the sea. Into these canals the fresh-water streams were con-ducted, and a pure running water thus kept up. Many of the sea fish, which spawn in fresh water, entered these canals and stocked the ponds with their fry, and, on their return to the sea, flood-gates were placed at the entrance of the canals, closing the passage, and while their posterity was growing, the fish themselves furnished the market."

These proceedings on the part of Lucullus were

imitated by the Roman patricians, at their villas, on
the borders of the Gulfs of Baïæ and Naples; and at
a later date, we have almost fabulous stories of the
cultivation of lampreys, and the prices realized by
red mullet of large size, and other fish. M. Jourdier
further adds a note, to the effect that this process
is carried on at the present time, in much the same
manner, on the rivers of the Basin of Arcachon,
"MM. Javal, Borsnere, and several large river proprietors, having there immense reservoirs, whence
they and their farmers draw very large revenues."
This may have been very ingenious on the part of
Lucullus, and is no doubt profitable to MM. Javal
and Borsnere, but if they only supplied the market
with the spent fish, which are on their descent to the
sea, I do not respect the taste of the purchasers.

Continuing his remarks upon the pisciculture of
the ancients, M. Jourdier speaks of the oysters of
Lake Lucrin, their cultivation having been originated
by Sergius Orata, in the time of Crassus. These
oysters were brought from Brindisi, and Sergius Orata
led the public to believe that the flavour of the
oysters was greatly improved by their residence in
Lake Lucrin. Hence they became shortly so popular,
that he covered Lake Lucrin with contrivances des-
tined for the breeding of oysters. The Lake of

Fusaro, a salt lake between the ruins of Cumæ and
the promontory of Misenum (the Avernus of the
ancients; the Acheron of Virgil) and of which I
may speak hereafter, furnishes another proof of the
skill which the ancient Romans brought to bear upon
this favoured art. As regards the practice of pisciculture later on and during the middle ages, we have
abundant evidences of the high estimation in which
it was held by the monks.   Indeed, it became a
matter of serious importance to them, from the supposed requirements of their religion, and the natural
difficulties which often presented themselves to the
providing of a supply of fish at all adequate to
the wants imposed by the fasts they observed.
M. Jourdier attributes to Dom Pinchon, a monk of
the Abbey of Réome, who lived in the fourteenth
century, the discovery of the method of breeding and
rearing fish by means of wooden boxes.   The ends
of these boxes were of wicker-work, and in the bottom
of them sand was deposited; excavations were made
in the sand, and the eggs of the fish deposited therein,
a gentle stream of water being then turned on, and run
through the boxes.   As far as I can understand this
method, which seems very simple, there is little difference between it and the plan at present adopted.

Subsequently to this, but more than a century ago,

we find another discoverer who appears to have practised the artificial hatching of fish, and in a very
complete and simple manner. This was Lieutenant
Jacobi, a German gentleman. His mode of proceeding is detailed in a series of papers published in the
Hanover Magazine, in 1763–4 and 5. This gentleman appears to have experimented upon various
kinds of fresh-water fish, and to have been successful with all of them. The plan he adopted for
hatching salmon and trout was to construct a long
oaken box, with fine gratings at the top and ends ;
to fill it partially with gravel, and, having procured the ripe spawn from a female fish, and fecundated it by mixing it with the milt of the male, to
deposit it in the gravel in the box ; and having then
placed the box in a clear running stream of a suitable
depth, he left the task of incubation to nature. And
this plan, with little alteration, is in use in the
present day. But the art, from some cause, for a
long series of years, fell into disuse, and was well-
nigh forgotten, when it was again revived in our own
time by two French fishermen of Bresse, in the
department of Vosges. It is to the genius and perseverance of these two men, Messrs. Gehin and Remy,
that we owe the re-discovery of this most interesting
and useful science. In their case the revival was

really an invention, since neither had ever heard of
the labours of Mr. Jacobi; and, so far, they are en-
titled to all the merit of the benefits arising from this
invention. Gehin and Remy were poor but intelligent
fishermen; and having, by watching the trout during
the spawning season, day and night, carefully noted the
whole process of depositing the spawn, it occurred to
them that this process might be carried out artificially,
and, thereby, vast quantities of ova, then yearly sacrificed (the fish being taken in the spawning season),
having been properly fecundated, and planted in the
river, might be saved, and little comparative damage
would be done to the fisheries by the practices unfortunately so much in vogue.

Having by experiments found that their plan was
perfectly feasible, they commenced their operations in
1842, although it was not until 1848 that their
claims to public consideration were acknowledged.
From that time, however, they successfully carried on
their process in various streams, both in France and
in Germany. About this time M. Coste, Professor of
Embryogenie in the College of France, took up the
subject, having been attracted to it by his experiments
on the embryos of fish; and hearing of what Gehin
and Remy were doing, he represented the matter to
the Minister of Agriculture and Commerce. The

attention of the Government was arrested. The
subject was considered, and finally it was determined
that a grant of 30,000 francs (1,250l.) should be
made, to create the establishment which subsequently
arose at Huningue. A brief description of the piscicultural establishment at Huningue may not, perhaps,
be altogether out of place here.

This establishment is situated at no great distance
from the Rhine, near the Rhine and Rhone Canal,
and in the neighbourhood of some large springs, the
water from which is used for the partial hatching of
the ova—for a comparatively small portion of ova is
really hatched at Huningue, the ova being sent
away to all parts of France, and even Europe, when
it is so far vitalized that the eyes of the embryo
within can be discerned. These eggs are then placed
in receptacles prepared for them, and the process of
incubation is completed.

The space covered by the establishment at Huningue
is about thirty-six hectares (about seventy acres), and
on this handsome buildings of considerable size are
erected, with suitable offices for the manager and the
attendants ; these buildings being disposed in the form
of a square, the middle or chief one containing the
offices. This is forty-eight metres long by eleven metres
wide. The buildings which stand at right angles to it

are two sheds, each sixty metres long by nine wide ;[1]
the other side of the square being composed of two
guard-houses.   In the centre is a court, with shrubs
and two small basins or reservoirs.   In the principal
building, on the ground floor, is a pavilion, in which
experiments which require particular care are conducted : over this are the offices.   The grounds are
laid out and interspersed with fish-ponds, ornamental
plants, flowers, &c.   These ponds are fed partly by
the Rhine water, and partly by the little rivulet of
L'Augraben, which traverses the grounds.   The spring
water is conducted to the buildings in which all the
operations are carried on by pipes entering the
building in three brick trenches, this water is then
raised to the proper height by means of pumps
worked by turbines, these turbines being driven by
the water of the Rhine.   In case of any failure of
the supply of spring water, the water of the Rhine,
which has been previously carefully filtered, can be
turned on to the apparatus.   Rows of cisterns, about
a yard in height, extend through the whole length
of the buildings.   These cisterns are each about ten
or twelve yards long, a yard in width, and eight
inches deep.   The ova is placed upon a glass grille, a
species of gridiron composed of hollow glass bars or

[1] A metre equals about 39⅜ inches.

tubes, placed closely together, the ends being confined in a sort of rack, made of wood. Each grille is placed in a small earthenware trough, glazed on the inside, this being the best preventive to the growth of confervæ. The troughs are placed crosswise in the cistern, and are about six inches wide and four or five deep. A tap at the head of each cistern permits the water to flow slowly over the range of troughs throughout the cistern. It will be seen that these troughs can, therefore, easily be removed separately

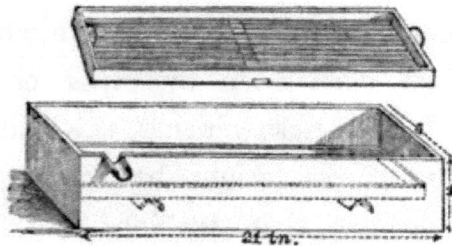

FRENCH TROUGH AND GRILLE.

for examination. In the building on the left operations requiring care are carried on. This building also contains brick basins for rearing. All these processes are carried on within the buildings, and thus extreme frost, or glare and heat of the sun is avoided.

The ova formerly was collected, by men who made a business of it, principally from the Rhine, the

Danube, and the lakes and rivers of Switzerland and
Germany. The tariff for collecting these eggs was
about two francs per thousand; but it was found that
immature eggs were sometimes sent, and a difficulty
of proper carriage resulted; and now the plan adopted
is as follows: The establishment is in correspondence
with all the principal fishermen at the above places.
When any of these fishermen have collected together
a large number of fish in a spawning state, they send
notice of it to Huningue, and one of the manipulators,
of whom three or four are kept upon the establishment, is sent to take the spawn, and bring it to
Huningue; a certain fixed sum being paid per
thousand for the various species of ova to the fishermen, who then sell the spent fish for food. The
eggs which are the most difficult to obtain are those
of the Ombre Chevalier; they cost the establishment nearly one penny each. All the best kinds
of fish which we have in England, and some
which we have not, as the Fera, the Huchen, and
the Ombre Chevalier, are included in their list of
operations.

When the applicant is successful in obtaining a
promise of spawn, printed lists are sent to him, one
comprising the fish which breed during the winter
months, and one of those which do not deposit

their spawn until late in the spring. Thus, two distinct classes of operations are kept alternately in progress.

The establishment employs several men constantly, at some periods of the year, of course, to a larger extent than others. In the winter, from a dozen to twenty men are required to attend to the various branches of the work; and, lately, even this number has been greatly increased, as the exportations of fecundated and partially incubated eggs since 1853 has increased from one million odd a year to sixteen millions. Save for the producing of food for the young fry, or as stock fish, or where new breeds or experiments are conducted, comparatively few fish are kept on the establishment.

The method of packing and exporting the ova will be explained in another portion of this work, so I need not further allude to it here.

Several millions of partially incubated ova of the various kinds of fish treated here are thus yearly sent to the various rivers of France. But large quantities of ova are also sent abroad to various parts of Europe, as the French Government are by no means selfish in respect to the benefits they desire from the art practised at Huningue.

The total cost of the buildings, &c. since 1853, has

been 265,186 francs, or 10,607*l.* The yearly expenses in salaries, travelling, carriage, &c. are 2,200*l.*, and it is calculated that Huningue produces *twelve live fish for one penny.*

Branch establishments are springing up all over France, under the patronage of that of Huningue. I think it is stated that there are already above a score of these.

Such is the first great piscicultural institution established in Europe; and if it is creditable to France that she should take the lead in this department of science, it is, on the other hand, discreditable to ourselves. We cannot plead ignorance of the existence of the fact of artificial breeding of fish; for, if we might be supposed to have overlooked all traditions, and even the more recent *Hanover Magazine* and Jacobi, we could hardly overlook Sir Humphrey Davy, who clearly details the whole process and its advantages in his "Salmonia." Compare, too, the relative interests of the two countries in all things relating to fisheries, and we have still further cause to feel how discreditable it is to us to *follow* in such a matter. But a malignant genius appears to have presided over the destinies of our fisheries, both internal and external. As the first maritime power, nothing connected with the improvement of our sea fisheries should be neglected. As an isolated power, relying much upon trade and upon other countries for our food, nothing which can produce a large and ever-present stock of wholesome food should be over-looked, but rather should such valuable resources be cultivated and improved to the very fullest extent. Yet, to our shame be it said, we do not even *follow* France in the establishment of a national institution of pisciculture. Small and solitary undertakings have been made by various river proprietors for their own benefit—these, for the most part, will be found collected and described in the Appendix—but any-. thing like a school of pisciculture has yet to be designed.

. Now, the reasons why pisciculture is not generally practised in this country are as follows :—In the first place, I must premise that there are a large number of persons who would willingly practise it, if they knew how to set about it, and who would gladly re-stock their exhausted fisheries by this means ; but they know not where to obtain fish spawn, or how to deal with it when it is obtained ; nor can they find persons sufficiently instructed to take spawn from the fish, or to set up apparatus for them, because there are not probably a dozen people in this country who know how to do so. An establishment similar

to that of Huningue is eminently required, not only
as a school, but whence, upon application, eggs of
fish, properly fecundated, might be obtained, and
such further advice and assistance rendered, as might
enable the applicant to carry out his desires, and
re-stock his waters.   I cannot but think that such an
institution might almost be made, to some extent
self-supporting, if once called into being ; and sure
I am, that, if such an establishment existed, there
is not a corner of these islands—indeed, we might
almost say, of the British dominions—where pisciculture would not soon become a most favoured and
profitable pursuit.   It need not, of course, be orga-
nized or carried out upon such a large scale as
Huningue, unless Government aid could be obtained.
Without such an establishment, it can hardly be
anything but a desultory practice, misunderstood,
unappreciated, and carrying with it few lasting or
notable results.

Before entering upon the subject of our inland
fisheries, I shall give a brief list of the principal fish
we already have in them, and of those which it may
be desirable to acclimatize.   Of each of these fish, I
shall treat according to its importance in the proper
place.

SALMONIDÆ.

The Salmon.	The Greyling.
Salmon Trout.	Powan,
Bull Trout.	Pollan,
Lake Trout (*Salmo ferox*).	Gwyniad, *Corregoni.*
Common Trout.	Vendace,
Charr.	

Of the common or coarser fish, we have—

The Eel.	The Gudgeon.	The Barbel.
Burbot.	Carp.	Bleak.
Lamprey.	Tench.	White Bait.
Lampern.	Roach.	Shad.
Sturgeon.	Dace.	Fresh-water Cray-
Perch.	Bream.	Fish.
Pike.	Chub.	

Fish which might be acclimatized—

The Huchen,	The Sander (*Lucio perca*).
Scandinavian Charr.	Black Bass.
Ombre Chevalier.	Maskinongè.
Ide.	Silurus.

Of the Corregoni—

The Fera.	The Lavaret.
White Fish (*Corregonus albus*).	

FISH CULTURE.

CHAPTER I.

OUR INLAND FISHERIES.

THE waters of our inland fisheries must be divided under two heads, viz. those which are capable of producing salmon, and those which are only capable of producing fish of less value.

As the salmon is of infinitely the greatest importance, I shall treat of it first.

In olden time there can be no doubt that salmon was far more abundant than it is now ; and we hear of its being a common practice of apprentices to have it entered in their indentures, in many places, that they were not to eat salmon more than a certain number of times per week ; and it is in the memory of many that servants have rebelled against being fed to a great extent upon salmon. It may be urged, in mitigation of this fact, that before railways were, the expense and difficulty of transporting salmon for long distances caused a vast supply of this fish to be thrown upon certain limited districts at times, and fresh salmon was thus often, for want of outlet for the sale, sold at as low a price as $1\frac{1}{2}d$. and $2d$. per pound ; and therefore the over-abundance in these particular districts, and the scarcity which exists there at all times now, is no fair criterion of the actual decrease of production. But while allowing all due weight to so reasonable a view of the case, we are fortunately enabled to set the point at rest by the irrefragable testimony of statistics. Statistics of the produce of various rivers have been kept for a long series of years, and we constantly find that some rivers have fallen to less than a half of their former productiveness ; in others salmon have been almost or quite extinguished ; and others, again, have suffered in various degrees. The great cause of this decrease is in every instance (save where mines and factories have utterly poisoned the rivers) the same, viz. that the stock is too reduced, a sufficient amount of breeding fish not being allowed to deposit their spawn in the rivers to keep up the stock.

Now, the general reader may understand the case if we put it thus :—Let us suppose a farmer to have a farm capable of supporting a thousand sheep. Let us further suppose him to be so supremely foolish as to yearly kill all his sheep indiscriminately down to some fifty, not excepting even those which are about to drop lambs, nor those lambs which are just born. It is abundantly clear that his fifty sheep will not

keep his farm stocked, and that ruin must in time
ensue. Yet still he goes on slaughtering, and won-
dering that he has not as many sheep on his farm as
he had formerly. This is somewhat the case on
many of our best salmon rivers.[1] But to make the
case still more clear to those unacquainted with
the salmon, save through the medium of a fishmonger, we must briefly trace the natural history
of the salmon as it is generally set forth and
accepted by those best acquainted with it. Salmon
leave the sea, and run up into the rivers, at all
times of the year, for the purpose, sooner or later,
of depositing their spawn in the shallows and fords
of the higher parts of the rivers. Some enter the
rivers in the spring, and push their way up from
pool to pool through the summer, until they reach
the upper waters, and these are of course the first
to spawn, and, being so early, they are infinitely
the most valuable fish to a river ; others, again, enter
the rivers in the summer; but the great rush of
breeding fish does not commonly take place until
about August or September (and sometimes they are

[1] The reasons of the decrease of salmon, and how it befalls that a
sufficient number of fish do not run up the rivers to spawn, will be
found in a practical detail of the modes of slaughter at present
employed against the salmon, in the Appendix.

later still), when on the first flood that comes down the river after they reach the estuary, they commence running up, being assured that there is plenty of water over the fords and shallow places for them to pass up to the best spawning-grounds.

The spawning commences with the early fish in November, and continues through December, and in late rivers even through January and February. Having deposited and covered their spawn or eggs in suitable gravel beds, in holes, or redds, as they are termed, which they burrow or scrape out for that purpose, they are so exhausted with the process, that they are quiescent for some time. Parasitic insects attack them in numbers, and the fish has not the energy to rid itself of them, and the salmon, or kelt, as it is called at this time, is often a foul and disgusting object, covered with sores. Lethargic, lank, and bad coloured, when taken from the water, it becomes very offensive speedily, and the flesh, which is white and flaccid, is mere carrion, and excessively unwholesome and repulsive. Yet thousands of these fish are caught by poachers yearly, and tons of them are exported weekly to France, or are smoked or kippered, and their nature being thus disguised, they find a ready market both at home and abroad. The destruction thus caused is

immense. An application has been made to the
Government, to prohibit this destructive and noxious
trade, by the Fisheries' Preservation Association, and
it is hoped that the Government will eventually do so.
When the kelt is in this state, it becomes necessary for
the fish to seek the salt water, partly to rid himself of
the parasites which are devouring him, and partly for
the plentiful food which he finds there. Accordingly
with the first fresh of water the kelt drops down from
pool to pool, until he reaches the sea. There, by
change of water and abundant food, he soon recovers
his strength ; and, in from three to four months' time,
he returns once more to the river, to procreate his
race, a splendid salmon, with flesh firm and red, and
increased in weight to an extent which bears no proportion to the growth of anything else in nature. A
kelt which will go down to the sea weighing 4lbs.
or 5lbs., will come back to the river weighing from
10lbs. to 16lbs.—from 2lbs. to 3lbs. a month being
a common rate of increase.

It has been asserted that the salmon can remain in
fresh water without ever going to the sea ; but I do
not know of a case where any material success has
satisfactorily attended on this theory. I believe
M. Coste, the great French pisciculturist, did try the
experiment, and that it proved a failure ; and I

believe it has been tried upon a small scale in this country, but with no encouraging result. There is said to be a salmon in some of the great American lakes very similar to ours, and these lakes being above the Niagara Falls, of course the fish cannot migrate to and from the sea. But it is also said that in these vast lakes, or inland seas, there are considerable tracts of water where salt springs prevail, and where the water is strongly impregnated; and it is further stated that the salmon, in obedience to its instinct, migrates to these tracts. If this be so, the fact is both singular and valuable; but I should much like to get some reliable confirmation of it, as I state it but on hearsay.

But we must return to the eggs deposited by the salmon. These, after remaining in the gravel for a period varying from 60 to 120 days, according to the temperature of the water, are at length hatched; but they do not come from the egg perfectly formed fish, nor do they entirely disengage themselves from the egg; for having cast off the shell, the egg still remains attached to the fish in the form of an enormous umbilical bladder. So cumbrous is this appendage, that the young fish moves but little more than is required to burrow under some stone of gravel at first, increasing in activity as the bladder decreases. During this time it requires no food, being sustained by the nourishment contained in the umbilical bladder. This, however, gradually grows less and less, as its contents are slowly absorbed into the young fish, and it finally disappears in about five or six weeks, when the fish is a well-shaped little creature of about an inch in length, and is capable of ranging about to look for food. At six months it is a lively active fish about three or four inches in length. At the age of twelve months, when it is from four to five inches in length, a singular change takes place. The fish, hitherto marked with transverse bands, and strongly resembling a young trout, changes its scales, and takes on it the brilliant silvery armour of a young salmon; a pretty bright and thoroughbred-looking little creature it is at this age, incessant in activity, darting at every small fly and insect that attracts its attention. When taken in the hand the transverse marks of the parr state have apparently disappeared; but if the scales, which come off in the hand at the slightest touch, be removed, the dark parr marks may still be discovered beneath them, proving the identity of the fish with the parr marked fish. When it has reached the stage above described it is called a smolt, and is ready for its first migration to the sea. With the first floods in April and May it begins to drop down the river from pool to pool and from stream to stream in large numbers, and finally reaching the open sea, it for a time is lost to us, and we know little of its habits save that it feeds voraciously while there on small fish and molluscs. Some authorities declare that this change and migration does not take place until the fish has achieved its second year, but others maintain that it takes place after one year. Experiment, however, has shown that to an extent both are right in their assertions, for it has been proved that while many, and by far the larger number, do migrate at one year, a considerable number do, nevertheless, remain behind, and stay in the river for another twelvemonth, migrating at the same period of the year as their more precocious brethren. Why this apparent irregularity should take place no one has yet been able to discover, nor has any rule or law whereby such an apparent freak is guided or accounted for yet been satisfactorily established. It having been supposed by Mr. Buist, the experienced superintendent of the Stormontfield experiments in salmon breeding, that this might have happened in consequence of some of the ova or milt being taken from grilse or salmon after only one journey to the sea, he took particular

care in the fall of 1860 to have the whole of the milt
and ova taken from full-grown salmon; but this
made no difference, for in May 1861, about the same
proportion of young fish left for the sea, and about
the same proportion also remained behind in the
ponds as usual. The smolt having reached the sea
remains there for a period varying from two to
four months, when it again returns to the river in
the form of a young salmon or grilse, having increased in weight to a wonderful degree, grilse
varying from 2lbs. to even as high as 12lbs. in
weight.[1] After its next migration to the sea as a
grilse kelt, it having spawned in the interim, it
returns to the river a full-grown and complete
salmon of from 7lbs. or 8lbs. to 16lbs. or 17lbs. in
weight, each year and each migration to the sea
increasing its weight considerably; but after the
first year or two it is supposed that its weight increases less rapidly; but on this point little as yet
has been clearly ascertained. Having now traced its
progress from the egg to the salmon, we must
return to the egg.

It must be manifest when the thousands of eggs

[1] I think it possible, as there is an irregularity in the period of
the smolts going to the sea, that there may be a like irregularity as
to their return, and that these large grilse may have stayed over
the twelvemonth in the salt water.—F. F.

which the roe of one female contains are considered,[1] that the produce of a very few pairs of salmon would be sufficient to stock a river, and doubtless they would be if a fair share of the eggs were hatched, and their contents reached maturity; but throughout its life the salmon has to battle with deadly foes, from the egg to the fishmonger's shop— from the cradle to the grave it has to run the gauntlet of one constant succession of remorseless enemies.

In the river, fish, birds, insects, and vermin assail the egg. Even whilst it is being dropped from the parent fish, shoals of small fry, dace, trout, and many other fish, lie in wait to secure and devour it. Water-rats and vermin of all kinds attack it after it is deposited in the gravel. Other coarse fish, and particularly eels, are supposed to rout up the beds, and commit the most serious devastation.[2]

[1] It is calculated that the salmon produces 1000 eggs for every pound of its own weight; thus, a 10lb. salmon produces 10,000 eggs.

[2] I have seen the small river lamprey hard at work on trout spawning beds; and the process is instructive. In groups of a score or so they search the beds and remove the stones. Fixing its sucker on a small gravel stone, the fish wrenches it from its bed, casts the fragment aside, and burrows into the hole it has made after the spawn. If the stone be too large for one to remove,

All kinds of aquatic birds, moorhens, water ousels, ducks, and particularly the tame duck, are of its worst enemies. When it is hatched, on emerging from the gravel, possibly before it can find shelter under a stone, it lies in a helpless state, hampered by the large umbilical protuberance, and it suffers again from foes of all kinds to the full as much as in its egg state, and from this time until it becomes a smolt it is alternately the prey of the trouts and of its own species; for the salmon when in the kelt state, being so ravenous, devours its own offspring with avidity, while gulls and many other birds of predacious habit hover over the shoals when on the shallow fords, and seize upon the young fish by hundreds; and even the angler, foul shame to him! scruples not to take them daily by the basketful, while whole bushels of them at a time are often taken by means of baskets and nets in the small mill-streams,[1] and they are even used in others to feed pigs with, so that scarcely one egg in a thousand ever produces a full-grown salmon. When it reaches the sea, the fish has a fresh series of perils to endure.

another will come and help him; nay, even four or five will unite their forces; and it must be a good sized stone which can resist their efforts. Of course the mischief they do is incalculable.

[1] In some places they are sent away to be converted into sardines.

Here fish of all kinds hunt and destroy it, and even when full grown it is the prey of the grampus and the seal; but these dangers from aquatic animals are comparatively few, for it soon becomes swift and powerful, and to a certain extent is able to take care of itself. In spite, however, of all this destruction, such is the amazing fecundity of the salmon, that were it not for the machinations of man— his worst enemy—sufficient of the species would still remain to fill our rivers almost to teeming.

The most dangerous and helpless part of the salmon's existence, therefore, occurs while in the ova state and until arrived at the smolt state. Fortunately here man has the power to protect it from most of the perils it endures when left to itself in the river, and at this particular point artificial propagation is a most valuable assistant.

In this country we have as yet had but few attempts made upon anything like an extended scale to put into practice the art of pisciculture. Perhaps those best known and of most importance have been carried out at Stormontfield, on the Tay; at Messrs. Ashworth's fishery on the Galway river, in both of which improvement of the fisheries was the object; at Mr. Cooper's fishery at Markree, near Sligo—here a fishery was altogether created; and on the Clyde, where a new fish (the greyling) was introduced. A fuller account of these operations will be found in the Appendix. The first of these experiments was conducted under Mr. Robert Buist, the second under Mr. Ramsbottom, and the last under Mr. Eyre, who is better known as the inventor of an ingenious machine for the transport of live fish to long distances.[1] In the two former instances boxes were used which were three-parts filled with gravel, the salmon ova being deposited in them; in the latter, boxes were thought objectionable, and the natural bed of the stream was preferred and the greater part of the ova of the greyling was accordingly deposited in the gravel (a short account of this operation was published in the *Field* by Mr. J. Briggs; a short extract from it will be found in the Appendix). In a conversation I had with Mr. Eyre concerning the natural bed of the stream and boxes, he stated it to be his opinion that the ova throve better under the above conditions, *i.e.* in the bed of the stream, because he imagined that there were certain gases percolating through the gravel below, which were very beneficial

[1] To these cases may be added the experiments of the Thames Angling Preservation Society, in adding to the stock of trout in these waters by artificial propagation, this process having been carried out at Hampton, under the supervision of my friend, Mr. Stephen Ponder.

to the incubation of the ova; and he had further
adopted this plan because he had known of failures
resulting from the use of boxes, and, as he appeared
to suppose, in a great measure from the absence of
these gases. I have, however, known the boxes to
succeed so often both with trout and salmon that I
am inclined to think there was probably some other
solution to the mystery, and perhaps the following
may be the reason:—When the ova is lying in the
gravel it is often attacked by predacious insects,
which prey upon it unceasingly; and the great aim of
the pisciculturist is to keep vermin of all kinds from
the ova. Now, if the gravel with which the boxes are
loaded is taken from the bed of a stream without
being either boiled or undergoing some other process
to destroy the animal and vegetable life existing
among it, it is impossible to prevent insects from
being placed in the box with it, as their eggs and
larva are mixed with and laid in the gravel itself.
When the gravel is transferred to the boxes these
eggs and larva in the course of time are hatched
and immediately commence preying on the ova. Mr.
Ffennel, the Commissioner of the Irish Fisheries,
found this a very considerable source of damage
to the stock of spawn which was deposited in
the experimental boxes at the Custom-house in

Dublin.[1] The best way, therefore, to meet this evil is to boil the gravel for about an hour and then to wash it thoroughly in a sieve before depositing it in the boxes.

There is also another very fatal cause of destruction to ova in boxes—viz. from the confined nature of the boxes any alluvial deposit which may be held in the water is much more easily precipitated than in the open bed of the stream itself, and a coating of this is often fatal to the embryo in the egg. To avoid this, even in the clearest streams, it is advisable to have a long and soft-haired brush and to gently sweep the gravel and ova in each box over every morning, so that any deposit may be disturbed and carried away by the stream. Even in the clearest streams, which never mud or thicken with rain and which may come from springs at no great distance, there are often matters held in solution which will deposit upon the ova, and from this deposit a conferva grows. Now, when the temperature of the water is low, let us say below 40°, this is not of so much consequence, as it can easily be disturbed and removed; but as the

[1] Mr. Brown, in his admirable little work on the "Natural History of the Salmon," as elicited by the Stormontfield operations, also bears testimony to the great destruction caused amongst the ova by the larva of the may-fly and by certain water-beetles.

spring approaches and the temperature of the water rises, the conferva, if left to itself for a time, appears to root itself to the egg and cannot easily be removed, and the eggs are often destroyed; consequently, the greatest care and precaution is required to prevent this. At Huningue soft brushes are applied to the eggs every morning *when necessary.*

The spawn of greyling is much smaller and more tender than that of salmon and trout, and is of course more liable to injury; but I think, with ordinary care and attention, there is little to be apprehended in boxes, while by depositing the ova in the bed of a stream the same amount of supervision cannot possibly be exercised, and they must be more open to the attacks both of birds and vermin. In one point greyling have an advantage over trout and salmon, viz. when these latter fish are spawning all the coarse fish which feed on ova are in the height of condition and actively looking about for food; when the greyling are spawning, save trout, there are few if any fish-enemies which are not themselves either engaged in the same operation or about to do so.

CHAPTER II.

ON THE ARTIFICIAL HATCHING OF SPAWN.

To give the reader a clear guide to the artificial
hatching of fish spawn, it is necessary that I should
describe the operations from first to last, and the
means employed; and as perhaps the best way will
be to describe minutely some particular set of operations, I shall take those of the Thames Angling
Preservation Society, which were carried on immediately under my eye from first to last, as I had
access at all hours to the apparatus. The operations consisted of two series or phases, applicable to
almost any fishery, one of them being conducted
out of doors and the other under glass.

I have always been an advocate for increasing
largely the stock of trout in the Thames, and for
the introduction of greyling into that river; and,
some years ago, I touched upon the latter subject in
the *Field*, and advised that it should be taken up.
It was slightly discussed at the time and dropped.
But I did not lose sight of the matter, and about

a twelvemonth after I introduced it again. Attention was again awakened, and an interesting discussion in the *Field* was the result. At that time the Thames Angling Preservation Society had not the privilege of preventing netting on the river, and consequently they were very naturally indisposed to breed fish for the nets to sweep away. Soon after this, however, the Honorary Secretary, Henry Farnell, Esq., applied himself to procure the abolition of netting, and finally obtained it. Once more I revived the subject, and the disabilities being removed, the Society took up the matter, and called a meeting to consider it. At that meeting it was decided that it should be at once adopted, and a sub-committee, consisting of W. Ponder, Esq., Frank Buckland, Esq., W. Lawrence, Esq., —— Hedges, Esq., and myself, was appointed to carry out the operations. By the kindness of F. Kent, Esq. of Hampton, we gained permission to make use of a small rill running from a spring, called the Christian Spring, through a meadow belonging to him, and the method of applying it, which I had proposed and sketched out, was adopted, and we proceeded to lay down our boxes. Unfortunately it was full late when we commenced operations, but we got on with tolerable rapidity. I must premise that there was a considerable fall in the run of the water, which was very advantageous to us ; nevertheless, the plan here adopted can be applied more or less to any stream. We first bricked up the little rill, so as to form a reservoir (1), and raise the water to a higher level we covered the reservoir in with a large stone, to keep out dirt and vermin, and placed at the lower end of it a zinc shoot (2), over which the stream

1, reservoir; 2, shoot through which water is discharged; 3, trough to catch the water before it passes into the box; 4, perforated zinc ; 5, shoot to discharge water.

flowed. Immediately under this we placed our first box, a fac-simile of which is given above. It was made of elm, four feet long and fifteen inches wide in the clear, and ten inches deep. At the upper end of the box, a projecting zinc trough (3) was fixed to catch the water, this trough being about three-quarters of the width of the box itself. At each end of every box a piece was cut out six or seven inches in width, and three inches in depth, and through these the water flowed into each box.[1] The top cut, which *first* received the water, being secured from foes without by being covered with perforated zinc through which the water flowed, and the further end one having a zinc shoot to deliver the water; and also a perforated zinc face, not only to keep foes out, but the fish in. Fastened over the cut in the lower end of the first box was a short zinc shoot (5), to convey the water into the next box over the corresponding cut, so that no water should run to waste between the boxes. Thus, when No. 1 box was fairly placed on a brick foundation, so as to receive the water in the zinc trough mentioned above, all that was required was to insert the shoot at the other end of the box into the corresponding cut of No. 2 box, and slide No. 2 safely and closely up into its place, and so on with Nos. 3, 4, and 5, &c. These boxes were then partially filled

---

[1] These openings were not carried all across the boxes, as the shoulders left made an eddy very favourable as quiet resting-places to the young fry when first hatched. If the stream be at all strong, artificial eddies should be created, by sticking small pieces of perforated zinc upright in the gravel at intervals along the sides and across the stream; behind these the helpless fry can be in safety.

with coarse gravel, of the size of gooseberries, and
some larger, even to the size of plums; for the more
irregular their shape the better, as there will be the
more interstices between them, in which the ova
can be hidden, and the little fish when hatched can
creep for safety. The gravel was at a level of about
an inch below the cut which admitted the water, an
inch depth of water being quite sufficient to cover
them. Each box was furnished with a lid comprising
a wooden frame-work, and a perforated zinc centre.
This lid was made to fit closely by means of list
being nailed on all round. It was padlocked down,
to keep out inquisitive eyes and fingers. Boxes in exposed places should always be covered in, if not with
coarsely perforated zinc, yet with fine wire netting, or
water mice will get in, and various birds, as moor-hens
and dab-chicks, will pick out the spawn, while a king-
fisher, should he discover them, will carry off the
fry by wholesale. The stream was then turned on,
and flowed steadily from box to box throughout the
boxes, and finally discharged itself by the end shoot
into the bed of the rill. It need not be imagined
that a full stream of water is necessary, for a small
amount of water is sufficient. Indeed, a flow of
water. say through a half-inch pipe, would be enough,
perhaps, though it is *advisable*, while the ova are

unhatched, to have more, so that there shall be more stream and movement in the water, and, consequently, less time for deposit to settle, so that we had on perhaps as much as a stream of three-quarters or an inch in diameter. When the fish are hatched, half that quantity would be preferable, as they are not well able to struggle against a stream, and would be carried down perhaps to the end box, and so against the perforated zinc face, where they would stop up the holes, and finally be smothered. The boxes were then properly steeped in water and seasoned, and being of elm the joints drew closely together after a while, and the boxes held the water without material leakage.

I may here describe how the ova was subsequently deposited in these boxes. The gravel was first placed at about one and a half or two inches below the cuts above described. The ova was scattered thickly over it, among the interstices of the gravel, to the extent of some 4,000 or 5,000 or more in each box. With a fine brush, such ova as might be too prominent was cautiously swept into some crevice, and the whole was then very carefully covered over with good sized gravel stones, tolerably flat and sizeable ones of say one inch, or one and a half inch square, being selected, the object being to

cover up the ova without squeezing or compressing
it. This, it is needless to say, is a delicate operation,
the depositing of the ova being very gently done with
a spoon ; the ova, being in a can or bowl of water,
whence it is lifted and deposited by the spoonful,
it is then spread as regularly and evenly about as
possible, thickly, but not heaped on top of each other.
Unfortunately, the first year, from some accident, we
did not procure the greyling spawn which we had expected, and some perch spawn was placed in the boxes
for experiment, and safely hatched in them. The
next trout season approached, and meantime I had
retired from the committee, though still taking every
interest in the proceedings, and visiting the works
constantly.

While talking one day with my friend Mr. Ponder
on the chances of heavy winter floods, often pre-
valent at Hampton, which might perhaps overflow
the boxes (as the meadow lay low and close to the
river), it struck me that it would be feasible for
him to erect an apparatus in his own greenhouse, as
a stream of clear water ran about ten yards from it,
and I suggested the idea to him, and without loss
of time he proceeded to put it into execution. A
well was sunk close to the stream, a force pump
erected, with a pipe from it communicating with

his greenhouse, shown at (*b*) in the section of the cistern, in which, on a lofty frame, a large slate cistern was placed capable of holding 200 gallons. Various experiments were tried, and Mr. Ponder found that this cistern would contain enough to allow a good stream, of about five-eighths of an inch in diameter, to flow for twelve or thirteen hours without running the cistern dry, so that it had to be

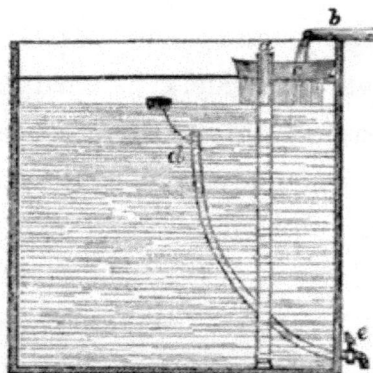

SECTION OF CISTERN.

pumped full morning and evening. The water was received into the cistern, through a large fine sieve (*c*) of double horsehair, and thus all leaves, insects, and foreign matters, were caught in it, and could not pass to the cistern; and as this sieve could be lifted off at will, the contents could be cast out from it every morning. Near the bottom of one end of the cistern was a stop-cock (*e*), by which the flow of the

water could be regulated; but the water was not
drawn from the bottom; a flexible pipe (*d*) was fixed
to the stop-cock *inside the cistern*, and this was floated
nearly to the top of the water, so that all deposit, &c.
sunk to the bottom out of the way, and did not pass
through the pipe. In the cistern there was, of course,
a waste pipe (*a*).

Immediately under the stop-cock, the first trough
was placed. These troughs were made of half-inch
slate. They were three feet long, seven inches wide in
the clear, and five inches deep, and were capable of
holding 3,000 ova each. Near the further end of the
trough was a small pipe, projecting from the side,
through which the water ran into the next trough.
The second trough was placed side by side with the
first, but about two inches lower. The water fell
from the pipe at the far end, travelled through the
second trough, and thence, through another pipe at
the near end of the second trough, into a third trough
similarly placed with discharge pipe at the far end,
the fourth having it at the near end again, and so on;
and thus there were arranged side by side, but in the
form of a flight of stairs, twelve of these troughs,
capable of holding some 40,000 ova ;[1] a waste pipe (*c*)

[1] It would have been just as easy to have had twenty troughs as
twelve if needful. With the twelve troughs some 40,000 ova were

GREENHOUSE APPARATUS.

from the last trough conveying the water into a drain.
I was rather in dread at first of sediment and con-

hatched in a space of about six square feet, or less even than that,
the actual space being about eight feet by three.

fervæ, and advised a filter to be applied. There was some difficulty in applying it in a mechanical point of view, and it proved fortunate, indeed, as matters turned out, that the temperature of the water did not permit the confervæ to grow. Had it done so, I fear that hardly an egg would have escaped—for being desirous of watching the entire process closely, my friend deposited the ova on the gravel instead of under it, and thus all sediment settled directly on the ova.

A rough filter, in such cases, is very desirable; one of the large-size flower pots, with side holes, every hole being corked but one, would, I imagine, answer well enough, a layer of fine gravel being placed in it first, say two inches deep; then a layer of charcoal, of the size of beans and peas, and then another layer of gravel; turn the water on to this, and, I think, a filter effective enough would be the result; a spare one should be kept at hand, to exchange in case of the filter getting foul.[1] Half of the troughs were filled to within an inch of the small delivery pipes, noted above, with fine gravel well boiled. The other half had, over beds of gravel not quite so high in the boxes, planes of slates fixed;

[1] With streams a bed or bank of sand and gravel will form a very tolerable filter.

these slates having holes bored with a coarse drill (about three to the inch), in order to deposit the ova one in each, much after the fashion of the racks used to hold shot on board a ship of war. It was merely an experiment; but as there was no advantage in it, beyond being able to tell the exact number of eggs, and it was rather a trouble than otherwise, added to which, the salmon ova, being large, stuck somewhat firmly in the holes, and it was difficult to dislodge them, I do not by any means recommend it. The French use a glass *grille*, or gridiron, made of glass tubes, placed closely side by side, and inserted into wooden frames at the end; on these the eggs are placed (*see cut in description of Huningue*, p. 9). These *grilles* are set up in small earthenware troughs, some two feet long and six inches wide, which are well glazed on the inside. I highly approve of the glazing, and think the earthenware troughs thus prepared, preferable to slate, and the glass certainly offers less hold to confervæ than any other substance. Excellent as these devices may be, and no doubt are, after much consideration I do not think that man's invention surpasses nature, and *I am firmly of opinion that the best plan to adopt is to place the ova under the gravel*, more particularly where much deposit is to be apprehended. If you want to inspect the ova by taking up a stone or two, and the use of a small glass tube as a siphon, the eggs, and even the fry, can always be drawn up into the tube with water, and inspected without injury. It is no doubt a very pretty sight to see the beautiful ova ranged thickly on the surface; but when a thick sediment covers them, which you do not like to interfere with over much, for fear of moving the ova too roughly (a liberty which ova will not permit of), the sight is not so cheerful; but, if this sediment merely settles on the upper face of the gravel stones, little or no harm is done, as you can sweep it away boldly, if it becomes too troublesome, without moving an egg or a stone. The conferva generally settles and roots itself on the upper face of a stone, preferring the light, and you may take up a stone foul with slime on the upper face, but bright as silver on the under side, and therein lies the safety of your ova. The water will not fail to find its way through the interstices; and all that the ova require is to be kept clean, cool, and moist.

A great deal of philosophy, much of which is somewhat imaginary, has been talked of the necessity for a rapid stream, and the constant aëration of the water. To exclude air altogether, or water altogether, would of course be fatal; a good stout coat of mud, for example, settled over the gravel, would, *perhaps*, though not absolutely to a certainty, consign the ova to destruction.   Ova may be, and often is, hatched in the damp moss, while being conveyed from place to place, if the eggs chance to be very forward; but, unless the fry is removed to water, it will scarcely survive its exit from the shell any length of time.   I have elsewhere said, that I could hatch salmon with a tumbler of water and a cheese plate, and this is no exaggeration; nor, provided the water were kept moderately cool, and changed occasionally, would there be the least difficulty in it, a running stream being by no means indispensable.   What current can there be in the natural condition when the eggs are three or four inches under the gravel?   Still, the water must not be allowed to become stagnant, as putrefaction begets putrefaction, and in nothing more quickly than fish ova.   When one egg goes bad, it turns white and opaque; putrefaction soon sets in; a peculiar starry fungoid growth radiates from it, and finally becomes much of the consistence and appearance of hair, or rather hemp.   Soon after, this touches the next egg, it adheres to it, and that egg in time turns off also. It is useless to attempt to clear eggs to which this substance has adhered; indeed, much harm may

result from the spreading of it to other and hitherto
sound eggs. The best way is to sacrifice at once all
that have come under its influence, or you can remove them to some spare tray *below* the other eggs,
where they may take their chance safely. So that
one of the most necessary duties to perform diurnally,
where the ova is exposed to view, is to remove, with
a pair of forceps, those which are bad. In this
respect, the small squillidæ or hopper, of the fresh
water, and insects of a like kind, are *said to be* useful
as scavengers, and their attacks on the live ova not
to be feared;[1] although the amount of stream *need*
be but small. I do not of course presume to say
that a fair amount of stream is not preferable in

---

[1] Of this I do not feel so certain. A few days since, while out
fishing, I picked up a mussel but recently dead. On looking into it
I noted a dark mass of something, which on closer inspection
proved to be a vast collection of these little hoppers, to the extent
of hundreds. The shell was almost full of them, and they had
eaten holes larger than themselves already in the mussel, which had
not been long dead, the flesh being quite fresh and free from smell
or taint. Indeed, I am quite inclined to think that they had
actually killed it. Still, I must allow that in the Christian-spring
rill mentioned above these insects abounded to profusion ; and
although we did our best to keep them out of the boxes, numbers
of them did get in. Yet I do not think they did any harm to the
ova. If they did, it was not to any great extent. If it be necessary
to keep them out, nothing but the finest wire sieveing will do it,
where they at all abound.

every way; but it is not, as I have said, an indispensable necessity.

The first ova deposited in the boxes was a quantity of the ova of the *Coregonus fera*, sent from France. This ova had been so long reaching Mr. Ponder, that it was bad, and soon became putrid, and the whole of it was useless. The next was some 4,000 of Rhine salmon. These ova were packed carefully in a box, in layers between damp moss, too great pressure being avoided, and large openings being left in the lid for air. They arrived in excellent condition—far better, indeed, than any subsequent ova that was received. A very small per centage of them were found to be bad; and the embryo was so far developed in the egg, that the eyes were very distinctly visible; and when in the water, close attention being paid to them, the embryo could often be seen moving in the egg. Soon after this, about 2,000 of common trout were received from Huningue. They were packed like the last, but had been longer on the journey, or had by some means become dryer, and a much larger per centage was found to be bad. They were, however, like the salmon, placed some on the gravel, and some on the slates. Meantime, small parcels of salmon ova came in from Galway and Clitheroe, and a small parcel of very fine trout ova from Lord Malden. I had pro-

cured leave for the Society from the Earl of Ports-
mouth, and Martin T. Smith, Esq. M.P., to take ova
from the Test—three or four other places, where I
had obtained leave, having failed us, from various
causes ; and Mr. Glover, a practical pisciculturist, of
considerable experience, and certainly the best manipulator I ever saw, was sent down to take the trout
ova. He returned from his first trip with some
13,000 or 14,000 ova, and subsequently obtained as
many more. Part of these were placed in the slate
troughs in the greenhouse, and part in the boxes in
the meadow. The Clitheroe salmon were also in the
meadow ; the Galway in the greenhouse. A small
parcel of ova of white trout also came in from Huningue, not in good order; and a smaller one still of the
ombre chevalier, or charr of Geneva ; and these last
were in very indifferent condition. Subsequently, we
obtained some 6,000 or 7,000 more of trout ova from
Samuel Gurney, Esq. of Carshalton ; and by the aid
of these, the boxes and troughs were as fairly tenanted
as was convenient.

The temperature of the water in the troughs, when
they were first filled, was as low as 38°. It rose gradually, as the spring advanced, until it reached 48°
and 50°. Of course, the atmosphere of the greenhouse
was much warmer than the outer air, and the slow-

running shallow water, by being exposed in the trays to its action, became warmer and warmer, as it travelled from tray to tray, until there was a difference of something like $2\frac{1}{2}°$ between the top or first tray and the bottom or last one. This difference in the temperature worked out very singularly in the hatching of the ova. With the first large batch of spawn got from Hampshire, three of the upper trays were supplied, these were alternate trays, with another tray intervening—thus the first tray supplied with this ova was No. 1 tray, and the last one, No. 5 tray. There was a difference of rather more than 1° between the temperature of the water in the No. 1 tray and the No. 5 tray; and this simple difference of 1° made several days difference in the period of hatching. The lower tray. began hatching first; then, after two or three days, the next above; and finally, after a further similar interval, the top one (No. 1). The temperature of the water in the boxes in the meadows was, throughout, several degrees higher than that used in the greenhouse.

When first the eggs were placed in the troughs in the greenhouse, they were of a delicate pale pink colour. In a few days, as there was no filtration, a dark brown sediment settled on them. This sediment gradually assumed a spongy confervoid

appearance, and finally covered the eggs entirely
with a thick mantle of black, slimy-looking substance, so that no one egg could be distinguished
from another; and, indeed, no one could have seen
that there were any ova there at all. We found,
however, on applying a soft camel's-hair brush to
them, that this matter was very easily detached
from the egg, and dispersed in a light gritty substance, leaving the eggs that had been beneath it as
bright and clear as when deposited. This was, of
course, very satisfactory so far. We attempted to
move some of the eggs from one tray to another;
but such a number of them died off, so rapidly and
instantaneously, while we were engaged in it, that it
was decided that they should not be disturbed until
the eyes became visible—showing that the embryo
within was alive, when the egg might be moved
about with safety. I may say here that ova should
not be moved without the greatest care and gentleness
until after the embryo has quickened. The best way
to carry it is to place it in a circular can, well covered
with water, the lid being thickly perforated, to admit
air; and, to avoid any shaking or splashing, the
person in charge of it should carry it in his hand. If
it is to be *sent* to a distance, a wide-necked bottle
should be filled with water to the bung; through the

centre of the bung an open tube should be inserted, and the bottle should, of course, be carried as upright and steadily as possible, avoiding all shocks which will disturb and destroy the organization of the egg, which at that period is very delicate;[1] but the safest and best plan is not to remove the ova, if it can be avoided, until the eyes are visible.

Of some 3,500 salmon ova, sent to the Thames Society, immediately after they were taken from the fish, from Galway and Clitheröe, scarce more than ten in a thousand hatched. Out of the 2,000 from Clitheroe, just twenty-five were hatched. It was supposed, by the gentlemen in charge of the operations, that the eggs had not been fecundated, or only

---

[1] The reader will understand this better by the following example :—If you take a bird's egg from the nest and shake it, and then put it back, that egg will not hatch, although it may not immediately go off bad, but may retain its fresh appearance for a long period. If it be shaken so violently as to destroy utterly the principle of life contained in it, then of course it will addle and become putrid speedily. If, on the other hand, it retains sufficient vitality to hatch, the chances are that it dies very soon after birth from the injury it has sustained in the egg ; or it comes into the world with some of the natural functions destroyed or disturbed, or a deformed thing. Deformities are very common in fish eggs that have travelled far. Even when the eggs of birds are sent upon a journey, they should be placed in sawdust, upright, with the small end downwards, and shaking avoided as much as possible.

partially so; but this hypothesis is not probable, or
how could the few that *did* hatch come forth? while,
if partial fecundation were supposed to be the cause,
the operation must have been more carelessly carried
out than is at all probable for so very small a proportion to have come in contact with the milt. It is
more probable that they were either too much shaken
or too closely confined from the air during their
journey, as the bottles were tightly corked.

The eyes are shown by one or two little black
specks, which become visible in one part of the egg,
in ordinary temperatures, about the fortieth to the
forty-fifth day; according to the state of the water, so
they may be looked for.

When ova is too roughly used, it dies off in a very
singular way; a small white speck instantly makes
its appearance on the egg. When you see this, you
may throw it away, nothing can save it. This speck,
in a very few minutes, spreads round the egg in a
white cloudy ring, and speedily envelops it; and,
in a very short time longer, the whole egg is of a
dirty opaque white. If left, it putrifies, and throws
out a kind of fungus, as before described.

The ova will often remain for weeks clear and
well coloured, even after the period when it ought to
have hatched. When this is the case, it has not been

properly fecundated by the milt of the male. Indeed, if the eggs get over from forty-five to fifty-five days without showing the eyes, there is little or no hope of them. Large numbers of eggs will often go bad about the same time, or at various periods, without any apparent cause; and when this is the case the probability is that they have been taken from an unripe fish, or one not in fit spawning condition. These also retain their appearance for a time, but go off at last.

Ova of salmon, it has been been generally supposed, require from 70 to 120 or 130 days to hatch; but this would, probably, be under water at very low temperatures, possibly from little above freezing to 36° or 38°, for a longer or shorter portion of that time, and thus the hatching would be much retarded. When placed in water of a higher temperature, however, ranging from 40° to 50°, this period is very sensibly abridged; and ova hatched in the greenhouse apparatus, as far as we could ascertain, did not exceed from sixty to seventy days—a material difference; and in this apparatus the water ranged from about 42° to 48°.

The bulk of the trout ova, however, hatched in from fifty to sixty days. They were afterwards conveyed down to the meadows, and placed in a spare box there, as the waters in the greenhouse troughs became

impure from heavy floods. These floods even swelled
the Thames, so that it inundated the meadows and
covered the boxes six or eight inches in depth; and
as at that period the young Rhine salmon had just
commenced feeding, and they could not be got at for
some days, a great many died, and many more escaped
from the boxes. Fortunately, the trout were uninjured; and the greater part of the stock were, in
due time, safely consigned to the Thames.

Trout ova are generally supposed to occupy about
the same period as salmon. I think, however, it may
be shortened somewhat. In the same water as noted
above, as I have said, we found the hatching range
from fifty to sixty days, while in the boxes placed
in the meadows, where the water is several degrees
warmer, trout ova hatched in forty-eight days, the
eyes being visible at thirty-five days, instead of from
forty to forty-five; and no doubt even this period may
be greatly abridged.[1] So that it will be seen, in this
instance alone, temperature could make a difference

[1] Mr. Fry, in his translation of the proceedings of the French
pisciculturists, states that salmon and trout ova in high temperatures are sometimes hatched even in thirty days. I have never seen
any hatched in so short a period, and certainly should prefer a more
moderate temperature. He states also that pike's eggs have been
hatched in nine days, the usual time being about three weeks.
Charr in from twelve to fifteen days, the usual time being here also
three weeks.

with salmon of from twenty to fifty days, and with
trout, even in the two apparatus employed here, there
was a difference of twelve days; so that it will be
seen that it is difficult to set apart any particular
period as the distinct time consumed in incubation. Trout possibly may be held to go a somewhat
shorter period, because the great bulk of them spawn
rather later than the salmon—vast numbers of trout
not spawning until February, and many even as late
as March.

On the 22d of February this year (1862), when
taking spawn in the Wandle, I saw scores of unspent
fish, and we could have obtained any quantity of
spawn we required. Water generally, therefore, will
of course be some degrees warmer than it was when
salmon were engaged in spawning, a month or so
earlier. I think it may be held, that while salmon
spawn from October to February, trout rather spawn
from November to March; of course, instances may
occur foreign to this rule. Trout take a longer time
over the operation, and take a longer time to prepare
the redd, or spawning bed, than salmon. And the
preparing of the redd is often mistaken by those not
well informed on the subject for the act of spawning;
and fish are thus often caught at this time which are
frequently a week or ten days, or even more, from

the actual time of spawning. The fish must be watched very carefully to hit the right time.

Greyling, again, occupy but a very short time. From the first week in April to the end of the first week or the middle of May, is nearly all the opportunity they afford to the pisciculturist;[1] and it behoves him, therefore, if he requires their spawn, to be watchful, and to keep on the spot, as a day or two's absence at the critical time—the occurrence of a sudden flood, however short, or any other such untoward event—may ruin all his hopes for the season, and lose him a whole year.

When a female fish is in fit spawning condition, the vent becomes slightly enlarged and of a reddish tinge. The ova, previously attached together by a membrane, become disconnected. Take up the fish and hold it first head downwards, then reverse it, and if the great bulk of spawn be seen to shift and drop as from one end of the fish's belly to the other, the eggs are loose, and the fish is ready to part with its ova.[2] If the bulk of the ova remain stationary, the fish is not ready. When a fish is in a fit condition to spawn, very little pressure is required to

[1] On any particular river, the spawning time often does not occupy above a week or ten days.

[2] See fig. 1 in the Frontispiece.

cause the eggs to shoot out in one continued stream, bursting forth like peas from a pea-shooter. When the fish is unripe, if you force out the eggs, you damage them by the pressure in the first place, and you rupture the membrane they are attached to in the second, so that blood will often be discharged with the ova, which is of course immature and useless; you may also seriously damage the parent fish. Whereas, if the ova be taken from her at the proper time—when the operation is over, it is not an exaggeration to say that she will dart off as actively as ever, and as if delighted to be rid of her burthen. The fitness of the male fish may easily be decided, as, if ready, the milt flows with the least pressure, and often without.

The method of holding the fish while expressing the spawn usually recommended is to hold the fish tail downwards, with moderate firmness, around the head, or rather shoulders, with the left hand, the belly being turned outwards and the back towards the manipulator's body, the points of the fingers and thumb being also turned outwards. The right hand then grasps the fish a little above the vent, so that the ball of the thumb is upon the belly of the fish.[1] The right thumb is then moved softly up and down

[1] See fig. 2 in the Frontispiece.

the belly of the fish, with a slight pressure on the down-stroke towards the vent, sufficient to express the spawn, which, if the fish be willing, will flow forth in a continued stream until the supply be exhausted. I say, if the fish be willing, because in some cases the fish will refuse to give out the spawn; when this is so, use no violent pressure, but exercise a little patience, and lay the fish aside for a minute or two, when in all probability its scruples will be overcome on the next application.

If the fish be a large one and struggles much, the assistance of a second person in holding the tail may be available, but it is of course very desirable that no hard squeezing or undue violence should be used whereby the fish may be injured and the spawn damaged. A flat, shallow, tin dish, such as it is customary to use for baking pies in, is the best receptacle in which to catch the spawn: it should be about half-filled with pure water. If the spawn renders the water turbid and thick something is wrong, and possibly the fish is not mature.

Before taking the ova from the fish the operator should collect in tubs of water about him the fish he intends to operate upon, and it should be his first care to see that he has a plentiful supply of mature male fish; it is advisable, indeed, to have more males

than females, for although a small portion of the milt
will doubtless fecundate the ova, yet it is very desirable that *enough* should be discharged to permeate
the water in the tin dish thoroughly. Indeed, when
the water is stirred to mix the milt and ova properly,
it should be of a cloudy milky-white.

Having then discharged the ova into the tin dish
and turned the female back into the stream, the operator should take a male fish and press forth the
milt on the water, moving the fish round about as he
does so in order that the milt may cover as large a
portion of the ova as possible. It will flow into the
water in a thin, milky stream. If one fish do not
furnish enough, he must take another and add a
portion of its milt; when he has enough he should
lay the fish aside and gently stir the water and ova
with the hand until the whole be thoroughly mixed
and every egg may have received its due portion.
The tray should stand for a few minutes that the
charm may have time to work, and then he must
pour off a portion of the discoloured water and pour
in gently a fresh supply of pure water from the
stream. Then he must pour off a portion of this
water and add more fresh water, causing as little
disturbance of the ova while doing so as possible.
This process should be repeated two or three times,

until the water in the tin is perfectly clear. During this process the operator should pick out any foreign substance that may have found its way into the tin, and when the water is quite clear the whole may be carefully poured into a small tin pail holding from half a gallon to a gallon of water, the pail being about one-third full of water. The lid of this can should be well perforated to admit air; it should be placed on one side where it is not likely to be upset. Meanwhile the manipulator can continue his operations, and when sufficient spawn has been collected for the purpose the can, which should not be more than half or two-thirds full of water, can be taken to any reasonable distance safely, *provided no rude shaking of it takes place.* To this end it is advisable that the person in charge of it should hold it in his hand *swung by the handle.*

I have here given the usual plan of taking spawn from fish. I will now give a better one—the one adopted by Mr. Glover, to whose skill I have already referred. In holding the female fish as already described, the spawn has to fall from the fish, pass through the air, and strike the surface of the water as it enters it. All this is unnatural and objectionable, more particularly the shock the ova receives when it strikes the water. Moreover, when thus held, fish are more or less able to struggle, which they will do, at times, violently. The better plan, therefore, is as follows :—

Place the tin dish before you, take hold of the fish by the head and shoulders, *with the left hand*, precisely as described above; hold it up tail downwards so as to allow the spawn to drop down towards the vent, then take hold of the fish with the right hand just below the vent so that the back shall be compressed by the fingers and the palm of the hand, leaving the thumb free to manipulate the belly of the fish ; slightly bend, or crook the fish, in order that the spawn which has dropped down towards the vent may be kept against the vent and not allowed to fall back from it when the fish is placed in a horizontal position ; press the belly of the fish into the water to the bottom of the tin dish ; the dish by this means greatly assists the grasp in holding the fish ; now rub the side of the thumb (the inside, not the ball) against the belly of the fish, just above the vent, pressing out the ova gently as in the first direction.[1] The ova in the neighbourhood of the vent will flow out freely, and when it ceases, hold up the fish again, tail downwards, to allow the rest of the ova to fall down to the neighbourhood of the vent, and so con-

[1] See fig. 3 in the Frontispiece.

tinue the operation until all be expressed. By this means the ova does not pass through the air, nor splash against the water; the manipulator has a firmer grip of the fish, and if the fish slips out of his hands it is not likely to fall and bruise itself. Occasionally it may be necessary, with a large fish, for a second person to hold the tail to prevent the splashing about of water and ova.

This plan is a little more difficult perhaps to acquire, than the one first mentioned, but it presents such manifest advantages that it is advisable to adopt it, and a very little practice makes the manipulator perfect in it. I have never seen it described elsewhere. The male may of course be held as in the former operation, the vent being on or just under the water.

I have been very minute in describing this process, as I am aware how difficult it is to understand such descriptions without actual manual example.

After the milt has been applied to the ova, a slight change in the appearance of the egg takes place—for a moment it becomes somewhat opaque. The contents appear as though troubled and in commotion. It then clears again, and a sort of inner ring or disc appears, which, doubtless, is the earliest indication of the yolk or embryo.

When you have conveyed the ova to the resting-place prepared for it, distribute it in a spoon, as before directed; and henceforth, until the period of hatching, disturb it as little as possible. Now and then you may desire to look at the ova, to see how it is progressing. If covered, remove a stone or two carefully; take a small glass tube, of about a third of an inch in diameter, and place the mouth of it over the ova you desire to examine; stop the other end with the forefinger, and thus, by suddenly removing it, the egg will be drawn up into the tube, with a small portion of water. Place the forefinger again upon the orifice, and turn up the end where the ova is, quickly, so that it remain in the tube. You may then drop it into an egg-cup or wine-glass, half full of water, and survey it at your leisure. A powerful glass, or the microscope, will enable you to note the singular and gradual development of the ova. Here-with I give a cut of the tube or apparatus used at Huningue for the purpose of testing ova and even small fish. It will be seen that with this it is not necessary to drop the ova, &c. into the glass or cup, but it may be held in the bowl part of the tube. If, however, a nearer view be needed, by turning the pipe upside down the contents can be discharged.

For some time, little change will be observable in

FISH CULTURE.

substance are formed. By degrees, these densify,
and, by aid of a strong glass, a thin whitish line
may be traced coiled within the egg. This is the
earliest development of the spinal column, and of
course it becomes more distinct as the animal becomes
more formed. And about the fifth or sixth week (in

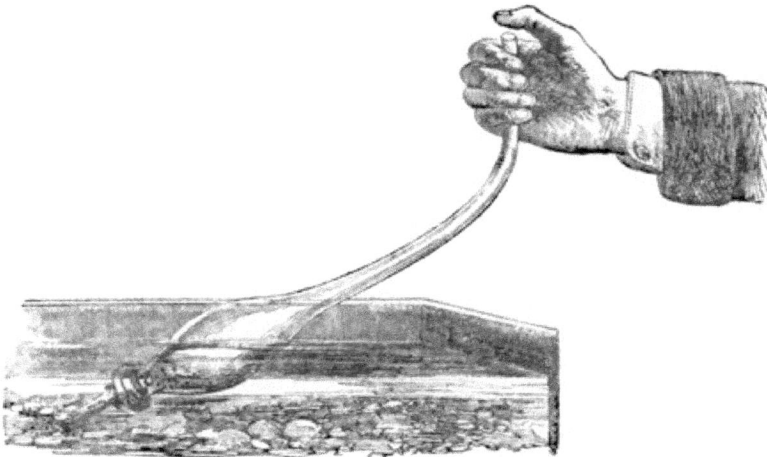

water of moderate temperature, we may say, usually
from the thirty-fifth to the forty-fifth day), a small
dark speck, probably, on close examination, two
black specks, will be observable. These are the eyes
of the embryo, the form of which may now be traced
almost by the naked eye. In a few more days, the
eyes become distinct, and the embryo may be discerned without the aid of a glass, moving and often

turning round in the egg. The articulation of the veins may be plainly traced. The pulsation of the heart and the rapid flow of the circulation can all be distinctly seen through the outer shell, forming a very wonderful and most interesting spectacle. In this stage, I have examined and watched the eggs for hours, interested and amazed beyond measure. The embryo being now alive, the eggs can be safely moved; a shock will not injure them. They require little more than to be kept damp, can be packed in wet moss, and sent to almost any distance with perfect safety—provided they be not placed, as some that were sent to the Thames Society were, near the engine-room or the funnel of a steamer, so that the heat dried up the moss, and destroyed nearly all the eggs.

From this time till the hatching, which takes place from a fortnight to three weeks or a month subsequently, the shell of the egg gradually grows thinner and thinner, and the motions and development of the embryo within more rapid and constant, and more clear and distinct. Some morning, when you visit your trays (if the ova be on the gravel, instead of under it), you observe a small reddish shining spot amongst the ova, rather larger than a pellet of ova, which catches the eye instantly; and on looking

closer, you find that one of your fish has thrown off
its shell, and emerged to life.

> " Take it up tenderly,
>   Treat it with care,
>   Fashioned so—"

No, not "slenderly," for a more unwieldy, delicate,
clumsy, welcome little stranger does not exist to
gladden the eyes of the delighted pisciculturist
withal. Now you have it in the little glass reservoir, with a drop or two of water around and over
it, under the microscope. How it wriggles and
kicks! what vigorous vitality is here, in this little
curious object! Now it is quiescent, and what a
wondrous spectacle is revealed to you! Is this a fish
or a new kind of tadpole? Verily, Sir Philosopher,
it is of fish, fishy—though not, perchance, fishlike.
Could this strange, helpless little thing ever become
the magnificent twenty-pounder, that takes you down
with breathless haste, with bending rod and whizzing
reel, stumbling and panting, full five hundred yards
of that terrific torrent, and flinging somersaults that
rival those of the deftest acrobat, gives you a full half-
hour's hard work and awful excitement in the Devil's-
hole below? Can this little marvel, I say, be the
foundation of that which has had hundreds of laws
made for it, thousands of pages of reports collected

on it, myriads of law-suits fought about it, Royal
Commissions without end imposed upon it; treatises
unnumbered, by the greatest lights of science and
genius, concerning it; by the catching of which
thousands live, and hundreds realize fortunes, *or the
reverse;* which millions feed on; and which should
be, if properly understood and treated, one of the
richest veins of our national wealth and subsistence? Verily, indeed, wonderful are the works of
Providence! Stay, let us look closer: a thin streak,
of almost transparent substance, about half an inch
in length, at one end of which two wonderfully
disproportioned eyes goggle at you through the
lens; at the other end the thin streak turns upwards,
and forms the tail part. From immediately below
the throat, and along where the belly should be,
depends a huge, unwieldy, umbilical bladder, larger
than the egg it has just emerged from. This bladder
is distended with a clear gum-like liquid. Up
towards the throat are a collection of those oily
globules before noticed, when in the egg state, just
over them. Stay; can that little red spot be the
heart? As I live, it is; and those thin filament-
like cords, extending from and branching off towards
the end of the bladder, are the veins. Now the red
heart pulsates; and the injected blood rushes, with

quick, steady action, through every vein—its progress
being distinct, even without the aid of the microscope, and as traceable as in an anatomical preparation. Second by second the pulsations continue—
But the animal is uneasy, and kicks and wriggles
again. Place it carefully back in its trough. There,
it darts to the bottom, ensconces itself between two
stones of gravel, and lies prone on its side. In a few
days you will be able to distinguish the rapid and
unceasing beating of its little fan-like pectoral fins.
But now glance over the trough, and haply you will
find three or four more red spots, indicating an increase in your registry of births. Here and there you
will, perhaps, see eyes very distinctly. Look closer.
They protrude from the shell; and this is how the
fish hatches out. Now the head is thrust out, and
the eyes stare forth at the wonderful world they are
about to come out into. The embryo wriggles, and
shakes the egg gradually; the shell splits across the
back, and the back is thrust out;[1] wriggle after
wriggle ensues; and the work of parturition goes on
with tolerable rapidity, A few more convulsions,
and the little fish springs forth from its shell, leaving

[1] Sometimes the tail protrudes first, and sometimes the shell
splits across the belly, and the bag shows first. In these instances
the struggles of the fish last much longer.

its empty case behind, and darts up to the surface of
the water in its glad joy at being released from its
prison, and then sinks slowly down again on the
gravel prone upon its side. Helpless innocent, what
a nice morsel now for a hungry trout! and what
havoc a monster of six ounces would make among a
hundred or two of them! Perhaps, after getting its
head out, it finds a difficulty in releasing the tail,
which is curled round the umbilical bladder within;
again and again it tries fruitlessly, resting between
each convulsion to concentrate its force for the next
effort. Take pity upon it; place your camel-hair
brush softly and caressingly upon it. See; there—it
is out. May you catch it, in return for your kind
offices, when it *is* a twenty-pounder.

At first the work of hatching goes slowly on; and
these early-hatched fish are seldom strong specimens,
very many of them paying the penalty of their pre-
mature appearance;[1] but as the days go on, they
increase in number, and soon a day arrives, as in
"the rise" of the May-fly, when Nature bends all her
energies to the work, and out they come by hundreds
and thousands; every hour, nay, every minute, adds

[1] The bladder should run back almost to a point behind in
healthy *young salmon;* when it is rounded too much the fish
seldom does well.

to the wriggling tenants of your trays, and after
another day or two but a sparse few lazy fellows,
indisposed to tempt their fate too early, remain to
come forth. Remove them to some spare corner of
an empty tray, that they may hatch at their leisure.
If you can remove the hatched fish to another tray
also, do so, that you may clear your lying-in hospital
of the useless egg shells that now thickly strew the
gravel. Little now needs to be done with the fish.

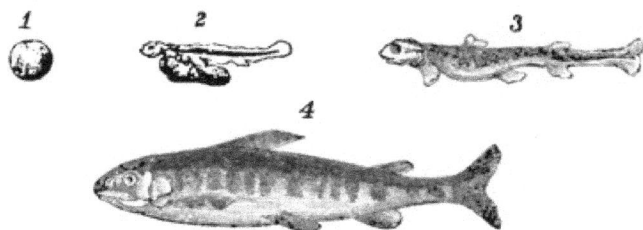

1. Egg with eye of embryo visible.
2. Young salmon just hatched.
3. Salmon having absorbed the vesicle.
4. Salmon three or four months old.

They will burrow under the gravel, getting out of
sight, and out of the light, which suits them not,[1]
as much as possible, gradually absorbing the large
bladder which attaches to them, the contents of
which afford their sole subsistence. In about six
weeks, as they grow larger, you will have to remove

[1] A slight awning over them as a shade is desirable.

a large portion of them to some other tray that they
may not be overcrowded. Little by little, the bladder
is drawn up and absorbed into the system ; as it
disappears the fish grows more and more active,
darting and skipping about the troughs. Soon no
trace of it is to be seen, and yet the water, if not
filtered (which it needs not to be after the fry are
hatched), will afford them for a day or two subsistence ; and now they begin darting to and fro
searching for more substantial fare, and they require
to be fed. And now it will be found that they require
still more room ; and if the pisciculturist does not care
as yet to turn them into the river, he should have
either a small shallow pond constructed, or a large
and long box or two of considerable extra capacity.
These boxes should be gravelled as the trays are, but
should be somewhat higher out of the water, as the
small fish are very active and apt to jump out. The
tops should be covered only with fine sparrow-
netting, to keep mischievous birds, as kingfishers, &c.
out, so as to admit plenty of light and air, and to
allow small flies to find their way to the water,
which at this period form the most natural, and by
no means a scanty, supply of food. About two inches
depth of water will be sufficient, and a fair but gentle
stream should be turned on. In places the gravel

should be heaped up slightly to make mimic shallows
for the fish to bask on, and at intervals of a foot or
eighteen inches along the side of the box should be
placed half bricks, these causing an eddy and a still
resting-place, behind which the little fish will shelter.
If this be not done, and the stream chance to be at all
strong, the weaker ones will be drawn down against
the lower grating, and will there, in all probability,
perish. A pond, of course, should be made upon
similar principles, and should be carefully gravelled;
but I do not hold with keeping the fry a day after
they are able to roam about and seek their own living.
I have heard people urge, that if the young fish
are turned into the river at that early age, they will
fall a prey to predaceous fish. It is possible that a
small per-centage of them may, but the remainder will
early learn to know their enemies and avoid them;
besides, in putting them into the river, the most
shallow places at the sides and the most sheltered
spots should be selected, and the fish should be
distributed in small numbers in such places as predaceous fish are the least likely to come and look for
them in. Added to this, the remainder will thrive so
much better in the wider area of the river, and will
grow so much faster, that this will counterbalance
any slight loss; and further, if the fry are kept until

they are of fair size, fed regularly every day, never
seeing an enemy of any kind what will become of
them when they are turned at once into deep water
amongst foes, without the preliminary and proba-
tionary life on the comparatively safe shallows, being
all unaccustomed to seek their own food or to see
enemies? They are far more likely to fall victims
then, and less likely to thrive on their own exertions, unless it be proposed to keep them until they
are beyond the size taken by pike or large trout, in
which case I do not think the pisciculturist would
be likely to repeat his experiment. The trouble and
expense of looking after and feeding the young fish,
too, is very considerable; so that, all things considered, it is far better to turn the fry in as soon as
possible. Still, it may be thought desirable to keep
some of them at any rate for a time, so we will consider their feeding. This at first must be done very
sparsely, or they will surfeit themselves if the food
be strong, such as liver or meat. A little ox or
sheep's liver well boiled, and ground or grated as fine
as possible, should be scattered to them daily. The
smallest insects or midge flies thrown in the water,
they will rise to and take with avidity. Various other
matters are used for their subsistence, amongst which
I will notice one or two only, since almost any

animal matter, if reduced to sufficiently small dimensions, forms food for them.

In feeding young fish, care should be taken to keep the bottom of the pond in which they are as clean as possible; as, if animal food is left in any large quantity deposited upon the gravel, it will of course putrify, and much damage the fish.

A few of the little squillidæ previously mentioned turned into the ponds then will be found useful in clearing up such matters, if no other means be practicable. While yet in the boxes, you may remove such refuse with the glass siphon which you have used to suck up the eggs; but this will be found a somewhat tedious process. Still, no means should be neglected which will tend to keep the water pure and clean. Lean meat, cut very thin, boiled well, and then macerated or pounded to a pulp, makes good food, the small fibrous particles being of the right size for the little fish to feed on. This kind of food is recommended in Mr. Fry's work.[1] If live food, however, be required, he recommends a variety of matters, as the flesh of coarse fish pounded small; and chiefly he advises that the ova of various of these fish should be procured and hatched, as the

[1] Published in New York, being chiefly a translation from the French.

young fry will take the embryo as soon as it appears with great avidity. One of his reasons for preferring this food is certainly a very valid one, and it is, that such food is not likely to die and putrify, and there is not much difficulty in obtaining large quantities of such spawn or in hatching it, as very many of the coarse fish are spawning from April to June, which is just the period when such food is required; as the fish increase in size chopped liver can easily be substituted. He also mentions the almost microscopic crustaceæ of the species Cythère, Cyprès, and Cyclops, which abound in stagnant waters, newly-hatched earth worms, &c. &c.

CHAPTER III.

ON THE TRANSPORT OF OVA AND FRY.

I MUST here say a few words on the transport of
ova and fry. I have previously pointed out the
period when it is most advisable that the ova should
be transported. The plan adopted at Huningue is
certainly the best known. A box is selected, a thick
layer of damp moss placed on the bottom, a sort of
bank or bolster of damp moss is then laid on this
around the sides, so as to leave a hollow in the
centre. In this hollow a quantity of spawn is placed,
sufficient of course to occupy it. The whole is then
covered with another layer of damp moss. On this
the same process can, if necessary, be repeated,
until the box is filled. Instead of a cover, strips
of wood are nailed across the top of the box, of an
inch or two in width, leaving spaces of a similar
width between to admit the air. *This side, of course,
is to be kept upwards.* In this manner the ova travels
safely for several days. I have already mentioned
the best means of conveying the ova *when only*

recently taken ; at Huningue, when such ova is dispatched, it is always under the charge of a special messenger, or of the guard of the train, who is properly instructed to pay it the requisite attention. In transporting the fry, little is required beyond an occasional change of water, and not too great roughness. If the fish has got rid of the bladder, it will be found advisable to aerate the water by means of a water plant or two being placed in the receptacle, as in an aquarium. By this means a large quantity of small fry may be carried to almost any distance.

Much has been written on the transport of salmon to Australia. Large sums of money have been spent upon hitherto futile attempts. Had I the charge of such an experiment, I should not pursue the plan which has been adopted, which is to place the ova, immediately after it is taken, in rather complicated trays filled with fine gravel, the apparatus being swung so as to alleviate as far as possible the ill effects of the rolling of the ship. Now, however carefully this may be attempted—nay, even if the rolling of the ship can be obviated altogether, which I very much doubt—there is yet another motion, the effects of which I do not think can be overcome ; and that is the thumping of the ship. Every one

knows who has been on board ship in a stiff breeze
the sensation caused by thumping. Up go the bows
of the vessel at an angle of 45°, under the effect of
one wave; down they go thump on the crest of
another. A huge wave comes like an avalanche
against the bows of the ship, and each of these blows
communicates a fearful shock and a jar to every
object animate or inanimate throughout the entire
vessel. No machinery that could be applied, that I
can conceive, would overcome the sensation of this
shock; and it is precisely shocks of this nature that
destroy the delicate system or organization within
the egg. Half a dozen such shocks would, I firmly
believe, go far to destroy almost every ova when
first taken from the fish; and although the ova might
still retain a portion of its vitality, and might remain
unchanged in colour even for weeks, I should place
no dependence whatever on the possibility of its
ever being subsequently hatched *to any good purpose;*
and even if a small portion should retain sufficient
vitality, in spite of all, to hatch out, I greatly doubt
if the proceeds would live a week. The dashing
against the gravel or the rolling may no doubt be
overcome, but the thumping I despair of. When the
eyes begin to be visible in the ova, these shocks
are of comparatively little importance. I don't, of

TRANSPORT OF OVA AND FRY.

79

course, mean to say that they are not still highly disadvantageous; but, *comparatively* speaking, they would do little harm. To show what an egg in this state can endure, I cite one instance mentioned by Carl Voght in his work.[1] He was once examining such an egg, when a sudden interruption caused him to drop it. It fell fully a yard on to the stone floor he was standing on, and rolled into a crack. He could not find it at the time, and there it lay out of water for two hours, after which he found it. Of course he did not expect to find it alive; nevertheless, on examining it, he found that the embryo was actually alive, and apparently uninjured. He replaced it in the trough, and in due time it yielded a healthy and active fish. I merely cite this instance to show what ova in this state can undergo. Now, instead of fine gravel, I would employ coarse irregular gravel, so that it might afford plenty of interstices. I would have the ova so far vitalized that the eyes might be seen. I would place it at a good depth in the gravel, cover it up carefully, and stretch tightly down over the whole a zinc wire netting, strengthened occasionally with transverse bars of

[1] "Künstliche Fischzucht," a very interesting little work on German fish, containing a chapter or two devoted to artificial incubation.

this metal hardened with tin. This would keep
the gravel in its place, and prevent it from shifting.
The ova would thus be kept deep and safely in the
gravel for a fortnight or more. I would also employ
ice freely to keep down the temperature of the water,
and retard the hatching as much as possible, as
every day gained is a day gained from the foul
weather usually encountered in the Channel and the
Bay of Biscay at the time of year when such experiments must be made. Light is disadvantageous to
the ova as well as to the hatched fry, and I would
therefore erect the apparatus in the hold, as near
the keelson and the centre of the vessel as possible,
there being less motion there, and space being of
comparatively far less value than between decks;
added to which, neither apparatus nor superintendent would be in the way in heavy weather, as they
are pretty sure to be in any other part of the vessel,
so that all operations could be conducted without
let or hindrance. The ova might be kept from hatching by a plentiful supply of ice for from a fortnight
to three weeks, and by that time comparatively fair
weather might be expected. Let us suppose the
ova hatched in the secure little chambers in which
they were deposited. Some few of the fry might
come up above the gravel; they, of course, would

stand their chance of being washed about; most of
them, however, would soon wriggle back again, particularly if a strong light were thrown on them.
Warm weather does not so much affect the fry as
it would the ova; so passing the Line and Tropics
would be robbed of much of its terrors. Moreover,
it would not, as in the ova state, accelerate the
development of the little fish; and for six weeks
they would lie perdue, quietly absorbing the bladder,
requiring neither feeding nor any great amount of
attention; and if the water could be kept moderately
sweet and cool, very little danger need be apprehended *to the larger portion of the fry.* By this time
the vessel will have progressed nine weeks on her
journey, and the fry would begin to appear; liver
can always be provided if the voyage should last
so long as for it to be necessary to feed the fish, and
proper receptacles could be provided for them. A
good many of the fish would of course be killed.
This we must always calculate on, but a large
remainder of them might, I think, be saved. Of
course the best means would have to be adopted to
prevent the undue wash of the water, from the rolling
of the ship, but the thumping would be of comparatively little consequence. In the system at present
adopted the ova would hatch long before the voyage

G

was out, and the fine gravel employed would afford
no safe holes and crevices for the fish to lie in while
absorbing the bladder. If they came above the gravel
they could not get back again, and would be washed
helplessly to and fro with every motion of the water,
which cannot be altogether overcome; and this, I
think, must eventually be fatal to them. I confess
that I have no very sanguine faith in the success of
the attempt to acclimatize salmon in Australia, if
what I hear of the rivers is true. The case seems to
be surrounded with very grave difficulties. The rivers
themselves may be suitable enough for salmon; but I
have heard that the mouths of them swarm with
small sharks, and what a famous meal one of these
of dog-fish size would make on a shoal of young
smolts entering the sea for the first time. If, however, a portion of them should still escape these
perils it would be but a small one, and the experiment would have to be repeated for three or four
years successively before any visible success could be
expected to attend it. The Australian Government
should set such a premium on these small sharks as
would make it worth the while of the fishermen to
catch them by every means in their power, so that
their numbers might be greatly subdued; and possibly a few years of active operations in destroying

both fish and spawn might render their numbers, to an extent, harmless.

The larger fish are, the more difficult it becomes to transport them. Fish so tenacious of life as eels, tench, carp, and even jack, may be transported with tolerable ease. The salmonidæ require more care and attention. In Holland, tench and carp are conveyed to market in wet moss, are put into tanks, and if not sold are re-consigned to the wet moss, and taken home again. Young salmon, trout, or grayling are more difficult to transport, particularly salmon. The best apparatus for moving the larger fish is Mr. Eyre's, fish-carrier. This is a large vessel, with a force-pump attached, by means of which air can be driven through the water.[1] Thus the water is kept aërated and wholesome. When this apparatus is put in action, fish that have previously appeared sickly, and

---

[1] The following description of the Fish-carrier is from the pen of Mr. Eyre himself :—

"The apparatus consists of a zinc cylinder, about three feet high and two feet diameter, with a strong iron handle running round the middle. To the top a small force-pump is attached, and by this fresh air is forced through a star-shaped distributor at the bottom of the cylinder. A ring-net, to bring the fish up for inspection, and a loose concave rim, to prevent splashing over, completes it."

The reader can extemporize a fish-carrier from a nine-gallon or smaller cask ; this must be thoroughly sweetened in the first place. Fasten a small force-pump down the inside, and from the bottom of

have been turning on their sides in an apparently
dying condition, instantly dive to the bottom and
assume their natural position. By this means large-
ish fish may be conveyed a considerable distance.[1]
Should one or two, however, really die, they should
always be speedily removed; this should not be
done by the hand, but by means of a small net:
indeed, the hand should not be used in contact with
these live fish oftener than is positively unavoidable.

An ingenious little apparatus has been made where
only a small quantity—such as a bait-kettleful of
baits, for example—is required. This is a gutta
percha tube, bent at the lower end and pierced with
small holes. Upon the upper end is fixed one of
those hollow india-rubber balls that children play
with; at the top of the ball is a small hole, on
this the forefinger is placed. The tube is passed
to the bottom of the bait-kettle. The india-rubber
ball is compressed suddenly, and an admirable little
force-pump, supplying plenty of air, is the result.

it carry a small leaden pipe across the bottom of the cask. This
pipe should be drilled full of small holes, and at every stroke of
the pump a shower of air bubbles rushes through the water. The
top should not be thoroughly open, but a large round hole should
be cut for air.

[1] Large grayling have been conveyed a distance of 250 miles
in it with little damage or loss.

Fish are of course far more difficult to transport when they are heavy in spawn, but by the above means, within the last twelve months, the Thames Angling Preservation Society have transported some 200 brace of fish, varying from half a pound to two pounds' weight, for distances of from 100 to 200 miles at a time, the greater part of them in that condition, with the loss of only four or five brace of fish; and these most probably were injured in the net or in the taking from the net.

The ova of salmon and trout may easily be hatched even in a drawing-room, by means of very simple apparatus, which need take up but little room and a comparatively small supply of water. All that is required is a small cistern, capable of holding a few gallons of water, with a small stop-cock to regulate the supply. Around this cistern may be coiled, as it were, in lengths, a small permanent gutter, or way, about an inch or two in width, and neatly gravelled. On this the ova can be deposited. Each coil or length, of course, must be lower than the other; and supposing the apparatus to be square, a little fall could be contrived at each corner. This coil or gutter, after passing two or three times round the cistern, should end in a water tank; and if the water tank be surrounded with a cooler, and furnished with

a small force-pump, the water can be forced up again
into the cistern, and may be used again and again.
If, however, the house be one well furnished with
water and large cisterns, a very small pipe to convey the water to the troughs or gutters, and another
to carry it off, will then be all that is necessary. Of
course, such an apparatus may be made as tasteful
and appropriate to the place it is consigned to as the
owner may please. Herewith I append a plan of
a parlour apparatus of my own designing. The upper
engraving shows the lid of the upper cistern (1)
open. The lower one has the cistern shut, but the
sides are let down to form a tray (7), into which the
young fish can be removed for rearing. The lower
cistern is shown by Fig. 2; the waste tap at (3),
whence the water can be drawn off; the supply
tap at (5); this either into the hatching trays (4, 4, 4)
or into the rearing tray (7). The force-pump is
indicated at (6); (8) is a waste-pipe screwed on to
let the water run from the rearing tray into the
lower cistern. Fig. (a) shows an enlarged end of
each of the trays with the lip, whence the water drips
into the next tray. This apparatus would be in
almost general use, I am fully convinced, if any establishment whence the ova could be obtained were in
existence. Many ladies as well as gentlemen would

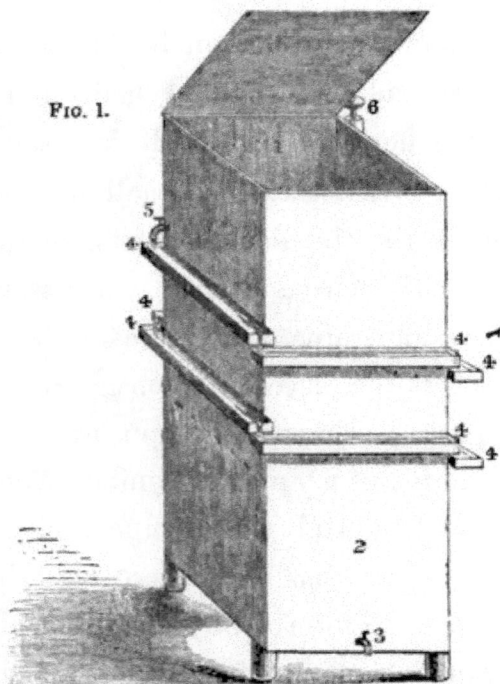

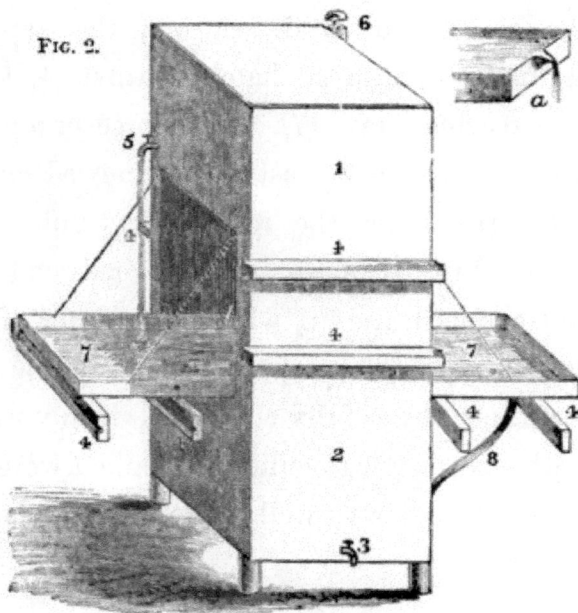

gladly enter upon so interesting and pretty a study,
and the sale of ova would, as I have previously
remarked, render such an establishment almost self-
supporting.[1] By the means I have described the
whole operation may be conducted. Nay, rivers even
might be stocked by the continuous use of a few
of these apparatus; nor do I think the day is far
distant when the present taste for aquariums will
in this way, as I have said, be turned to a useful
purpose.

There is one other species of contrivance used occasionally in France I believe—the floating apparatus.
I have never seen one of these in operation, but
can easily conceive that they possess many advantages in some places. Mr. Fry mentions them. They
are composed of wicker or basket work, somewhat
after the shape and fashion of the baskets called
by poulterers and others "flats," save that they are
shallower and of course more carefully made. The
ova is deposited on a grille within it, and the basket
is floated on some gentle but clear stream, the basket
being weighted just so much as to allow an inch of
water to flow over the ova, and being kept in its

---

[1] The Commissioners of the Irish Salmon Fisheries have hatched
a considerable number of salmon ova, and tried some interesting
experiments, in their offices at the Custom House in Dublin.

place by guys anchored to the bottom or sides of the stream. This is a very useful invention no doubt in some places, particularly where there are no small streams, as it can be floated about from place to place without difficulty or danger to the ova.

Note.—Since this last Chapter was written and the proof-sheets revised, news has arrived of the failure of the last attempt to transport salmon by means of new ova to Australia; and although we have not the precise facts of the experiment, yet I feel that the failure bears out much that I have advanced in the foregoing Chapter. The great point which it will be necessary to discover is, whether any of the ova ever became so matured as for the eye to be developed; that we have yet to learn.

CHAPTER IV.

THERE is not an insect or small reptile that inhabits
the soil beneath us, the air above us, or the waters
around us, that is not food for fishes in a greater or
less degree. Worms of all kinds, flies of all kinds,
grubs and larva of all kinds, cockchafers, crickets,
leeches, snails, humble-bees, young birds, mice, rats,
frogs, beetles, all serve the turn of one fish or another,
and so in turn help to produce food for man. Black
beetles, for example, often looked on as a nuisance in
houses, are caviare to the trout; and I have seen two
or three trout devour a panful of them with the
greatest avidity. Nay, I have seen a wary old six-
pound stream trout, that had been tempted with
every conceivable variety of bait, succumb to the
temptation of a black beetle. Small frogs, just
emerged from tadpoleism, they rejoice in exceed-
ingly; and I have even seen them take young toads,
though some do repudiate the taste on the trout's

part. Nothing living comes amiss, but doubtless some kinds of food agree with them far better than others. But we know very little on this branch of the subject. It is dreamland to us, with a very little ascertained waking reality. What do we know even of the various breeds of the same species of fish, save the bare fact of their existence? What do we know of the food and conditions most favourable to them? Consider the trout. Can any fish display greater diversity or variety of size and value than trout? And how do we account for it?

Trout in one stream will be much larger, firmer, redder, and better shaped than in others. This may, in a measure, be owing to *the greater abundance* of food; but I have every reason to believe that it proceeds quite as much from the kind of food that they are enabled to obtain. In some rivers and lakes we find the trout large, handsome, red, and vigorous fish; in others, we find them small and meagre; nay, even in the same lake the fish will be influenced in a strange way by locality, so much so that the very breed even appears to be different. It would seem difficult to account for this peculiarity upon any other hypothesis than that of food and the nature of the water and soil around them, and yet the fish appear to be a totally different breed; and it

certainly appears possible that the character of the
fish may have changed by degrees, through succes-
sive generations, and owing to being bred and fed
in a different manner from the other fish. I have
placed trout from one stream into another, and after
years could very easily distinguish them from their
compeers of the stream, but I doubt if their progeny would show and retain their special charac-
teristics.

Few experiments of any note have been tried in
the feeding of fish, this being as yet almost untrodden
ground; but I once heard of an experiment being
tried in the following manner:—Equal numbers of
trout were confined for a certain time by gratings to
three several portions of the same stream. The fish
in one of the divisions were fed entirely upon flies;
in another, upon minnows; and in the third, upon
worms. At the end of a certain period, those which
had been fed on flies were the heaviest and in the
best condition; those fed on minnows occupied the
second place; while those fed on worms were in
much the worst order of the three. The probability
is, that had another pen been set off, and the fish
fed with a mixture of all three species of food,
the fish in it would have far exceeded any of the
others in weight and condition.

Some rivers notoriously produce larger trout than others, although the character of the soil they flow through may to all appearance be very similar. I will instance two, both of which are tributaries of the Thames—the Chess, a branch of the Bucking-hamshire Colne; and the Wick, a little stream running through High Wycombe. I select these two streams because they are only some ten or twelve miles from each other, and because they are as nearly as possible of a size. Now, it is generally supposed that the very best and most fattening food provided by Nature for the trout is the may-fly, or green-drake. This fly abounds in profusion on the Chess; it is rarely if ever seen on the Wick—in fact, it may be said not to exist there. The minnow, likewise supposed to be most excellent and nourishing food for the trout, is also a stranger to the Wick; or if it exists there, is not found in any considerable number. Sticklebacks and millers' thumbs are found in places, though they do not abound in all parts of the stream. The caddis, or case grub of the smaller flies, however, is very abundant; and in some of the hatch holes there are a considerable quantity of leeches.

On the Chess a trout of two pounds would be a very fine one, the fish averaging from half a

pound to a pound and a quarter. On the Wick it
would be an ordinary fish; indeed, they are not considered fair takeable fish under a pound and a half.
They are often caught of four and five pounds, and
I have known them to run up to seven or eight or
even ten pounds; and this in a small stream, little
more than a good-sized brook, is a most astonishing
size; for not only do these fish acquire this unusual
weight, but they arrive at it very rapidly indeed.
I have had many opportunities of knowing how they
will increase under favourable circumstances, as one
of the fisheries on the stream belonging to a friend
of mine was on one or two occasions almost destroyed by bleach and tar water—some forty or fifty
brace of fish being all that were saved: none of
them were over two pounds, and yet, in two years,
many of them had grown to six and seven pounds'
weight.

Taking the Wycombe fish as a breed, I may say,
that they are the heaviest and thickest fish, for their
length, it has ever been my lot to see; while the
colour of the flesh of a good fish, instead of the ordinary pale pink of a really well-conditioned trout, is
often of a deep red, much redder, indeed, than that of
salmon. On the other hand, the Chess fish are not
particularly handsome, shapely, or well coloured.

Here is a point well worthy the consideration of those who wish to take up the science of pisciculture. What particular species of food can it be which not only makes up for the total absence of the may-fly and minnow, but so feeds the fish in this admirable little stream, that there is no river, large or small, which I have ever seen in all England, can for its size equal it in production? What, then, can be the particular food that fattens them so rapidly?

My own impression is, that the fresh-water Pulex, or Screw, which I have previously referred to once or twice, has not a little to do with it, for these insects abound in this stream even to profusion—to a greater extent, indeed, than I have ever found them in any other brook. The trout feed upon them voraciously; and it is a very common thing to find in the trout a mass of these insects, half digested, and as large as a filbert. I have seen the trout picking them off the walls, which pen the stream in some places, as rapidly as a child would pick blackberries from a hedge; and I am induced to think that this insect has, as I have said, much to do with the fineness of the fish; and the more so, because, when I have found it to exist in any quantity, I have invariably observed that

the trout are of fine size, and in unusually good
condition.[1]

In lakes, also, it is a very common thing to find
the trout in one lake large, bright, and well fed, and
in another, very similar in appearance, and perhaps
only a bare half-mile distant from the other, they will
be long, black, and lean, with heads out of all proportion to the thickness of the body.   In another,
probably but a similar distance from the first two,
the trout will be abundant, but very small, though

---

[1] These insects of course thrive better in sluggish than in rapid
water, though they do well enough in either when there are weeds.
They are peculiarly well-adapted for lakes; and were I owner of a
lake, I would leave no stone unturned to introduce them in large
numbers.   Where the streams are too rapid for their plentiful production, it would be by no means a bad plan to make here and
there (where the situation of the soil and the banks suited such a
plan) small shallow ponds, supplied with water by means of
a small pipe, and having an exit to the stream.   In these the
requisite kind of weeds might be planted, a stock of these little
insects turned in, and some kind of offal or other food (see
page 22) occasionally being cast to them, and the insects left to
thrive and increase.   They would of their own accord make their
way into the stream, where they would afford excellent food for the
trout.   Other kinds of insects might be also placed in such food-
breeding ponds, where they might propagate and multiply in safety.
By such a method as this almost any amount of the food best
suited to the trout might no doubt easily be produced.   *For if we
increase the stock of fish, we must, of course, if their size and weight
is to be kept up, grow food for them somehow*, and this seems not to
be a difficult plan.

bright and well coloured. These varieties, I have every reason to believe, are caused partly by a difference of water, produced by the absence or presence of certain plants, these of course giving a difference of food. To exemplify this: I remember some years since, while fishing in a wild part of Donegal, near the little village of Ardara, coming upon a cluster of small lakes. The trout in some of these lakes were small, bright, and very plentiful; in others, they were of a good size, but not handsome. But in one of the lakes, a small one—a mere pool, of perhaps a couple or three acres in extent—my attendant informed me that the trout, though of a dark colour, owing to the darkness and depth of the water, were large and well shaped, often running up to five and six, and even seven or eight pounds' weight. But the lake was what is termed among anglers "a sulky lake," that is, the fish very rarely rose well at the fly, and probably it might be fished a dozen times without producing a single fish, though there were times and days, if the angler chanced to hit upon them, when very good fishing might be had, and when the lake appeared alive with fish. I fished the pool, however, and had the good fortune, by sinking the fly, to take one of the trout, a strong well-shaped fish, though somewhat dark in colour, and of two pounds' weight.

H

We also caught specimens of the fish in the other lakes, and the difference between the fish I have already mentioned. While fishing the small lake I accidentally allowed my fly to sink to the bottom, and on pulling it up again with some difficulty I brought up a large piece of a thick moss-like green weed, with which the bottom of the pool appeared to abound. On examining this weed more closely I found it swarming with a variety of insects, chiefly water-snails, the small crustaceæ that inhabit fresh water, and large quantities of the caddis of some considerable fly. The abundance of food thus found at the bottom of the lake fully accounted not only for the large size and good condition of the fish, but also for its being a sulky lake, or for the trout not paying much attention to the flies upon the surface of the water. For they had no difficulty in procuring any quantity of food they needed at the bottom, without swimming hither and thither to seek it, or giving themselves the trouble to come to the top. Colonel Whyte also mentioned a fact somewhat of this nature, some time since, in the *Field*. He related, that wishing to improve the size and condition of his fish in a small lake, he cast into it a bushel of the small crustaceæ, which are often found on water weeds. These increased rapidly, and as they did so his trout increased in size and improved in condition wonderfully; but it is also fair to say, that they became much shyer of rising to the fly. Probably the reason why the fish sometimes rise well to flies, and not at others, in lakes like those of Donegal (which are by no means few), is owing to the fact that the abundance of caddis at the bottom may be undergoing some transformation, into flies perhaps, which ascend rapidly to the top of the water, and the trout are thus led in pursuit of them to the top of the water, where the insects rest, and are easily captured. If anglers, being aware of this fact, made some little study of entomology, so far as to know about the time when these insects undergo their transformations, they might not be induced to seek such lakes so often in vain. In the instance I have noted the lake is deep, and the water dark; and the fish at the bottom, engaged with ground food, do not see the flies at the top.

Again, I will instance the fish in Loch Leven which grow to a large size, and are almost always in superb condition. The bottom of the lake, in places, is grown over with a peculiar weed; in this is found a great variety of insects, chiefly crustaceæ, as small snails of various sorts: the lake also abounds in the more minute entomostracæ. Large quantities of both are often found in the stomachs of the trout when

taken. Here sport with the fly is generally good,
because the lake is shallow and clear, and the fish
see the fly well. In other lakes, again, where these
species of weeds, which form the harbour and subsistence of these insects, are wanting, it will usually
be found that the trout are small, or, if large, ill-fed
and meagre. I know also a small lake in Wales,
where the fish never take a fly until after dark, when
fish from 2 to 3lbs. weight (an unusual size for Wales)
may be taken. This lake abounds in leeches, and
the trout are very fine in it. A quarter of a mile off
is a similar lake, in which trout do not thrive at all,
and, indeed, are seldom found; while about a mile
from it are one or two small lakes, in which the trout
do not average three ounces. And yet the character
of the lakes, and the soil in and about all of them,
are apparently precisely similar.

It cannot be doubted that the condition and size of
trout, as well as other fish, depends almost wholly
upon the supply of food, and I think I have shown
that the particular kinds of food are also a great
desideratum. Now, it being known that particular
kinds of weed are favourable to the production of
these certain species of insects, what can be easier—
when the soil is favourable to such a measure—than
to transplant a sufficient quantity of these weeds, and

the larvæ of the insects which will almost always
be found to abound in them, from one lake and from
one stream to another? For example, with respect to
the squillidæ so often noted, what could be easier
than to transplant weed? This would serve as food
for the large fresh-water muscle found in almost all
waters, and it would serve as food for the squillidæ,
which in turn would serve as food for the fishes. It
may be said, with regard to some lakes and streams,
that they are so gravelly or rocky, that the weeds
would hardly thrive in them; but it is seldom indeed
that some nooks and corners do not exist, in or about
the banks of lakes and streams, where there may be
found sufficient soil, which, with a slight admixture
of the natural soil, and a judicious planting of these
weeds, may not be made to grow them to some small
extent; and the weeds, once introduced, will gradually
increase year by year, forming their own soil, and
naturally producing those requisites which are the
most favourable to their production. Of course judgment must be exercised in carrying out such experiments, quite as much as would be exercised in the
introduction or cultivation of a new food-producing
plant in agriculture. We acclimatize every species
of agricultural plant, and examine its qualities and
capabilities, for cattle or for ourselves; we study

the soil suited to it, &c. &c. ; we have shows and
prizes for the best specimens of agricultural pro-
ductions, and thousands of persons assemble to note
and study them ; but who ever thinks of acclimatizing
an apparently worthless water-weed?

Now all plants, even to the meanest looking weed,
have their uses for man ; and among the fauna of the
world, there must be many which would be valuable
to us in the light above indicated. We have received
one from America—the alsinastrum. This weed has
hitherto been a terrible nuisance, growing so rapidly,
as to fill up and choke our smaller rivers, in many
instances, in an incredibly short time ; but it might
be that this weed, so troublesome and so difficult to
eradicate in the south, would be a great benefit to the
hill and moor lakes of the hard north. Hardy water
plants, in which insects can thrive, are greatly wanted
there; and it might be found that the introduction of
the alsinastrum, and its attendant insects, would have
a very favourable effect on the size and flavour of the
trout found in such places. I do not of course say
that this *is* so, but I merely suggest the possibility
in order to point out how such designs could be
carried out. It would in time become a very interesting and valuable fact, to hear that Mr. So-and-so had
brought home a new water-weed, favourable to the

production of certain water insects, from Timbuctoo or elsewhere. There must also be a vast number of water insects, which would prove valuable to our fisheries if introduced, provided we knew all about them.

I think I have said enough to show that there is here a very wide field for discovery. Here is, as I have said, a new world—a new science to be learnt. The modern taste for aquariums and vivariums has given us some small insight into how to cultivate those plants which we already possess, which are the best calculated to *look well* in the tanks, but we do not study even these to discover the natural duties and uses for which Providence designed them. We do not in a like manner work out the properties of the insects that inhabit them; and what could be more easy, or would be more interesting, to the entomologist, than to watch the changes and the habits of the various insects that people the waters—to see the most delicate, beautiful, and harmless little flies in creation spring from curious and ungainly grubs, or fierce predaceous larvæ, changed in form as in nature, to a degree altogether unaccountable! What wonderful and interesting processes would not reveal themselves to the curious observer! How encouraged he would be to note each new fact, and record every phase of each transformation! How valuable, too, would be the study of the peculiarities of these beautiful and almost microscopic entomostracæ! What more delightful to the student than to know that he is making new discoveries most beneficial to mankind, and which will be connected with his name in future generations! There is no part of creation uninteresting, without its uses, or which does not possess its benefits for man; and there is none, therefore, which is not worthy of his most earnest attention. Those who first study this science, and who first discover its hidden secrets and virtues, will deserve well of their country. For it is well said that "he is one of the greatest benefactors to his country, who makes two blades of grass grow where one grew before;" and, therefore, he who makes two, twenty, or two hundred fine fish, where one wretched starveling only grew before, will assuredly not be very far behind in his deservings.

Leaving for a time the subject of water weeds, let us take other views of the necessaries for good water cultivation. Many rivers are starved, in a great measure, for the want of a few trees and bushes along the banks, as foliage is one of the great purveyors and providers of food for trout, and therefore, in many places now destitute of it, and where the trout run small, it should if possible be encouraged. Some people are very fond of introducing minnows into their rivers and lakes, to form food for the trout; but minnows, unfortunately, feed on precisely the same kinds of food as trout. They are incessant rangers in search of food, and very voracious, and before he becomes food in his turn, probably a minnow of fair size will, at a very low calculation, have devoured twenty times his own weight of food; and, consequently, instead of benefitting the trout, the minnow has deprived him of nineteen times its own weight of varied food. This quite accounts for the fact of trout often rather falling off and deteriorating in lakes into which minnows have been largely introduced. Vegetable-feeding creatures are rather what are required than such as feed on other insects.

CHAPTER V.

ON THE CROSSING OF BREEDS OF FISH.

AND now we arrive at another valuable consideration
—that of crossing of breeds.   There can be no doubt
much may be elicited here.   In some rivers, the race
of salmon and trout are naturally small, and without
apparent reason.   In Scotland, for example, there
will be four rivers running into the same estuary,
and the breed, shape, make, and size of the fish of
every river will be distinct and different.   In some,
the fish will be long and thin in shape; in others,
short and thick.   In some, they will scarce ever
exceed twelve or fourteen pounds in weight, and in
others they will run up to twenty, thirty, and even
forty pounds, if allowed to exist for a reasonable time.
Now, here it is evident that the rivers themselves
can have little or nothing to do with the growth of
the fish, since the great feeding grounds wherein the
fish grow and increase their weight, at a rate out of
all proportion to that of any other created creature,
are identical, being the broad sea; since salmon

never increase their weight in the fresh water after their first trip to the sea, but rather fall off and deteriorate. Why is it, then, that, enjoying these feeding grounds in common, some thrive so much better and faster than others? It cannot be doubted that it is in the nature of some breeds to increase more and faster than others, even as a Hereford or Norfolk steer exceeds a Welsh or Highland stot, feed him and breed him how, where, and when you will. We have discovered how, by the crossing of breeds of animals, we can get those which carry flesh best, and increase the fastest, upon a small amount of food. How easy it would be, therefore, having discovered the same thing with regard to fish, to transplant and cross the breeds of salmon and other fish, until we found that which is most valuable and suitable to our various rivers. Here is another branch, then, of the science, scarcely inferior in importance to the last, but of which we know literally nothing. Is it not a surprising thing, that a people whose interests are so vast in the elucidation of such questions, should be content to remain in ignorance of them, and should make scarcely an effort to obtain enlightenment on them? It would be very difficult to compute how many millions a-year are lost to this country by an ignorance of pisciculture. Indeed, it may with some

reason be said that the absence of proper understanding and cultivation of our waters *may* make just the
difference between wealth and poverty.   Having said
so much, it is needless for me to pursue this fruitful
and important theme further.   It is to be hoped that
public attention will be awakened, and that we shall
speedily begin to make up for the time we have
so lamentably lost.   The subject of hybrids is one
which, in the present state of knowledge we have
upon it, possesses an interest in a scientific point
of view rather than a practical.   That hybrids can
and have been produced we know, but whether they
are any improvement on the breeds of fish we already
have, seems to be a highly problematical question.

CHAPTER VI.

CONSIDERATIONS ON THE BEST KINDS OF FISH FOR RIVERS.

THE next points to be considered are the wider dissemination of the best kinds of fish we at present possess, and the acclimatization of other kinds found in foreign countries, but at present strangers to our waters.

The best fresh-water fish we have are salmon,[1] sea-trout, charr, trout, grayling, burbot, lampreys, perch, eels, flounders, and gudgeons. The tench, carp, bream, dace, roach, jack, &c., require the assistance of cookery, not exactly to make them acceptable, but to make them, let us say, palatable or agreeable.   It is difficult to explain the exact estima-

---

[1] I do not enter here upon the means whereby salmon may be more widely disseminated, and why they are not more plentiful; the subject is too large for a place in the body of this chapter; it is so much a subject by itself, that I have so placed it in the Appendix, where those who may be more specially interested in the legal matters, methods of fishing, and other recondite matters which beset the salmon question, may find it.

tion of these fish; but we may say, if not very well
cooked, one would not select any of them for choice
at a Blackwall dinner, though they all afford wholesome food to some one. Now, there are many trout
streams which are not, perhaps, capable of supporting
salmon to any extent, but which might be greatly
improved in value by the cultivation of the spawn of
the sea trout. Of course, in speaking of sea trout, I
refer to the white or salmon trout, and not to the
Erioc, Grey, or bull trout, which is, compared with
the other, almost a worthless fish, being a bad riser
for the angler, and, though excellent while small, an
indifferent fish for the table when of any size—two
bad qualities not usually found in the salmon trout.
Moreover, although a handsome fish, it is so destructive, that, wherever it appears in any quantities, its
far more valuable congener, the white trout, and even
the salmon, gradually disappears before it. I recommend it, therefore, to be kept down, as we keep down
vermin in our shootings. The Tweed and its tributaries suffer heavily from a mistaken preservation of
it. There are many of our salmon rivers which might
easily afford good sea trout, if they were duly introduced and encouraged; for the addition of sea trout
will not in any way interfere with any other fish, and
they are next in value, both for the table and the

sportsman, to the salmon itself; and any one who has seen the manner in which some of the western Irish rivers and lakes swarm with this delicious and game fish, will readily testify to the value of such an introduction.

At the charr I must pause. Charr at one time were far more plentiful in this country than they are now. Their principal habitat was the Lake district, when few of the lakes were without them. They are found also in many of the Irish lakes, in one or two in Wales, and perhaps some half-dozen or a dozen in Scotland. The practice, however, of taking these fish in such vast quantities in nets, when they come in and to the shallow water to spawn, has terribly thinned them, and in many lakes they are very much reduced in numbers. The charr, moreover, is the most delicious fish that inhabits our fresh waters, and this, too, is another incentive to its destruction. There are, according to some ichthyologists, several species of charr; according to others, they are simply varieties. It is believed by some that the charr of Windermere, Llyn Bodlyn, Lough Melvin, and elsewhere in the British Isles, is identical with the Ombre Chevalier. I shall touch on this point when I come to the consideration of Lakes. It is tolerably certain, however, that it is not identical with the great Northern or

Scandinavian charr, as it is said never to be found in
rivers. The habits of the northern fish appear to be
widely different from those of its southern congeners,
since it is constantly found in abundance in rivers,
not alone near their junction with lakes (whence, as
it might be supposed, they had migrated for a time),
but altogether away from lakes. Lloyd, in his "Scandinavian Adventures," mentions taking them with
the fly again and again in rivers ; and he is supported
by very many other authorities. The Rev. F. Metcalf,
in "The Sportsman in Norway," also speaks of catching charr. He mentions one of six pounds, which
he caught with a minnow close by the falls upon the
Mallanger river. Further up the river, he again
speaks of catching large numbers of splendid trout,
charr, and greyling ; and to show that they are not
confined to particular localities, he afterwards speaks
of quantities of charr being taken in the nets *near the
river's mouth, where the water was almost brackish.*
Now, the consideration for us is, not that our charr
are *not* found in such places, but that the Scandinavian
charr *are ;* and as there is no great difference in the
character of many of our rivers and lakes, and many
of the Scandinavian rivers and lakes, it certainly
appears to me that we might easily transplant and
add this very delicious fish to our faunæ with con-

siderable advantage. I have had specimens of this fish sent me from Iceland, of two and three pounds' weight. There they appear to inhabit the most rapid streams, and they take the fly and bait as freely as the trout. They were sent to me by Mr. Hogarth, the lessee of the river Sog, where they abound in profusion. The Scandinavian charr is constantly taken of seven and eight pounds' weight, and, according to Mr. Lloyd, of sometimes double that weight.

The Ombre Chevalier, as I have said, is supposed to be distinctly a lake fish; so I shall not treat of it here, but take it under the head of Lakes.

The grayling needs little description. It is a very well known fish, abounding in many of our rivers and streams. As an edible fish, it certainly comes next to trout, and even contests the palm with it when in good season in the months of October and November. Where the rivers are small, it would be advisable, if it is to live with trout, to establish a breeding apparatus to keep up the trout stock, the expense of this being but small. For although the grayling is a very handsome addition to a trout stream, and finds fly-fishing for the angler at that period of the year when the trout does not, it is a great ground-feeder. Its habit, at times, is to grub or rout like a pig in the gravel and sand; and hence, as they

I

are in the best order when trout are spawning, they
are apt to destroy the spawn and to greatly reduce the
supply of that valuable fish. I am compelled to own
that I believe they do a good deal of mischief, and
there is often a strong, and not unfounded, prejudice
against them. They might possibly be made, in many
of our mixed rivers, to take the place of worse fish,
such as barbel, &c. They are, however, being somewhat widely spread about over the country, owing to
the popular discussions which have taken place upon
them in various publications. In Scandinavia they
are said to abound, not only in the streams, but in
many of the lakes—a fact unknown in this country,
but very worthy of note.

Much has been said of the burbot. In Switzerland
and in Scandinavia, this fish is very highly esteemed,
and travellers who are among "the initiated" make
as great a point of having *lök* for dinner as the
cockney does of whitebait at Blackwall. Having par-
taken of it, I can quite concur in any strong eulogy
on its merits. It is a very firm, white, and delicious
fish. The head somewhat resembles the fin of turbot,
and the liver is not equalled as a delicacy by any
other morsel of fish substance in existence. Had it
been known of old, the Roman emperor would certainly have added burbots' livers to the great dish of

nightingales' tongues. It is a shy fish, hiding in
holes and under roots or stones, and is of no value to
the sportsman, as it is seldom taken, save on a dead
or night line. It abounds in many of our rivers, particularly in those of the midland counties, and can
easily be distributed; but as it is a very voracious
fish, and a great burrower in the soil, it is almost
doubtful whether it would not devour more spawn
than it is worth. This, however, is, I am bound to
say, but a mere conjecture on my part, which remains
to be solved by further experience.

The Lamprey. This is unquestionably a delicate
fish for the table, though, from some cause or other, its
popularity, once considerable, has so far diminished
that it is hardly ever seen in a bill of fare nowadays;
and in many places so strong is the prejudice against
it, partly, perhaps, owing to its ungainly appearance,
that the inhabitants refuse to partake of the lamprey,
and cast it away when they chance to capture it. The
appearance of the flesh is somewhat similar to the
burbot, but with a peculiar and indescribable flavour;
is also inferior to the burbot in respect to the head
and liver; indeed, the liver of the lamprey should be
very carefully removed before cooking, as it is of so
bitter and unpleasant a flavour that it is apt to taint
the entire fish. There are various ways of cooking the

lamprey; stewed, however, it presents the best dish for
the gourmand, but it is also potted and made into pies.
It can hardly, however, be considered a fresh-water
fish, as it spends the greater part of the year in the
sea, merely entering our rivers, like the salmon, in
the months of April and May, to deposit its spawn;
until this process is completed, it is in good condition.
It is seldom taken in the sea, however, and when
taken in the river is caught in any way but that
of angling. It grows to a considerable size, and often
weighs three or four pounds. Its power of fixing
itself to stones, or wood-work, or any other substance,
by means of the sucking apparatus at its mouth,
enables it to surmount any fall or obstacle to other
fish. It is found in almost all our larger English
rivers, as the Severn, the Trent, and formerly it was
common in the Thames; in the latter river, however, it is rarely met with now; the sewage and filth,
probably, has driven it elsewhere. In the Usk it
abounds, and in some of the Scotch rivers, but in
neither case will the natives use it as food. In the
Shannon it is also plentiful.

There is another species of lamprey, much smaller
in size, called the lampern, which resembles at first
sight a grig, or small eel; it is of some ten or
twelve inches, or even more, in length. This little

fish comes into many of our rivers in vast shoals with the earliest winter floods; the water being somewhat fresher and clearer at that time, it has not yet abandoned the Thames, but is taken in large quantities at the various locks; at Teddington and Moulsey are the chief fisheries. The fish are chiefly bought up by the Dutch long-line fishers, who cut them into short lengths to bait their spillets with, the bait being very tough and bright and attractive to the fish. Large sums of money are often shared amongst the Teddington fishermen as the produce of their fishing. The fish are taken in wheels or basket-traps, similar in make to the eel-traps, and many thousands are often taken in a night. As a table fish they are certainly liked by some people. At Worcester they are potted and are in great request. I cannot say that I appreciate them, however, having tried them in various ways. They are rather rich and strong-flavoured. Perhaps, when marinated (baked in vinegar, bay-leaves, and spice), they are better than in any other form; and even then I do not think the operations of the Dutch fishermen deprive us of any considerable delicacy. One thing I may say in connexion with them, viz. the offal makes capital bait for barbel. Certainly it is not nearly so desirable a table-fish as its larger congener.

Perch, Eels, and Flounders are sufficiently well
known to render any description needless. Perch do
not improve in flavour by being placed in waters
having mud at the bottom; but a good stream-perch,
from a clean gravelly water, is by no means a fish to
be despised.

I may perhaps here mention by far the best way
to cook a perch. Take a good-sized fish and lay it on
the gridiron precisely in the condition in which it
comes out of the stream, merely cleansing and drying
the scales. Do not cut off either the fins or the tail,
or the juices exude from the cuts; when it is sufficiently done, take it off the gridiron (do not let it
cool), make a slit down the back, insert your knife
under the skin and lay aside the mass of scales and
skin, which will come off like a suit of armour,
leaving the firm, white, juicy flesh exposed; rub the
flesh well over with a slice of butter; pepper and
salt to the taste. Flake off the flesh with your knife,
leaving the skeleton and *interior* intact, and you will
find the meat as delicate and delicious as that of any
fish that comes to the table. The ordinary methods
of cooking perch utterly destroy the firmness, juici-
ness, and flavour which it naturally possesses.

Perch should certainly not be introduced into
waters that support trout or salmon, as they are

voracious devourers of small fry, and in such places are not worth their keep.

Eels are, perhaps, better suited to muddy than gravelly rivers, though they abound in both and are better flavoured when taken from the latter. They are great spawn-eaters, and it has been questioned whether the eel pays for his keep owing to this circumstance. In some salmon rivers I have seen the lower pools in a perfect boil, when the eel fry is migrating, with the constant rising of the fish as the small eels wriggled along the top of the water; so that the salmon, if the eels be supposed to be destructive to them, exact summary vengeance. Their ravages, however, amongst salmon and trout spawn cannot be very extended, as the spawn is in the gravel during *the winter*, and eels are not active in frosty weather. They may, and no doubt do, however, take a heavy toll from the helpless fry when first developed in the spring, as the eels then begin to move. The Dutch keep eels out of their carp ponds as much as possible, as carp spawn in June and the eels would no doubt do damage to them. Eels, where they have the chance, migrate about autumn in large numbers towards the brackish water near the rivers' mouths, the water there being usually several degrees warmer than that higher up. Those

which remain behind, as many do, bury themselves
in the mud or seek some hole in which to hybernate.
It has been questioned whether the eels that so migrate do so *for the purpose* of spawning in the brackish
water. I think it cannot be questioned that they do
spawn there, else whence those countless myriads
of small eels, which, under the name of "eel-fare,"
migrate from the brackish water up to the fresh in
many of our large rivers? I have seen them in the
Erne, in Ireland, pushing their way up even from the
sea in countless millions, early in the month of May.
I think there can be no doubt that they spawn as
well in the brackish as the fresh water, but that if
they have the choice they prefer the warmer or
brackish water. Of late years, in the Thames, they
have not had this choice, owing to the filthy water
about London, in which it has been proved that eels
cannot exist. The consequence has been the dis-
continuance of "eel-fare," once a very striking and
remarkable sight, on the Thames. The eels have, it
would seem, from this circumstance, greatly diminished in numbers; and whether it be that the fresh-
water spawning is not so favourable to their increase
as the brackish, or whether large numbers of eels still
migrate and die in the foul water, or that, getting
down with a flood to aid them, they *do* spawn and

the fry are killed when they reach the foul water, I am quite unable to say; but I have little doubt that when the Thames is once more purified "eel-fare" will in time again recur to it. Eel fisheries are in many places very valuable. The fishery on the Erne realizes many hundreds of pounds a year. Any eulogy as to the excellence of the sharp-nosed eel for food is needless. There are three kinds of eels known in England: the broad-nosed, the sharp-nosed, and the snig. The former is a coarse worthless fish, but is not very plentiful; the last is a very local species, found chiefly in the Hampshire Avon.

Flounders for the most part are not taken in any very great quantity above the tide-way, and may therefore be encouraged as far as possible. They are an admirable table-fish, however they may be dressed. A Thames flounder is held a special delicacy; large quantities were formerly caught from Battersea to Hammersmith. Of late years, however, the sewage has affected even them, and they are scarcer. In most of our brackish and tidal waters it abounds.

The Gudgeon is a most delicious fish, although a small one; it is scarcely less delicate than the smelt. Few gravelly rivers in the midland counties are without them. They serve, too, not only to furnish an excellent dish for man, but a *pièce de resistance*

for all fish of prey.   The fact is not generally known,
but gudgeon will thrive very well in ponds.   In one
of the ponds in Richmond Park—the largest of the
Penn ponds—it has been the custom of the anglers
fishing there, in order to save the trouble of carrying
home their bait-kettles full of water, to empty their
cans and turn the remainder of their live baits
into the pond.   Many of these baits being at times
gudgeon, they have lived and thriven, and have bred
so freely, the keeper has informed me, that on the
gravelly part of the pond it is easy to catch four,
five, or six dozen in an hour or two; but the
gudgeon thrives equally well in a muddy pond and
in even stagnant water, for I once emptied my bait-
kettle into a horse-pond; there were about a score
of large gudgeon in it, and they bred rapidly in the
pond, so that in a year or two there were abundance
of gudgeons of all sizes.   I have, however, never
eaten gudgeon from a muddy pond, and therefore
cannot vouch that they would retain their delicate
flavour.

After the fish above noted I should place the pike
or jack, the dace, tench, carp, bream, roach, and,
lastly, chub and barbel, and I would take occasion to
draw a strict line here.   None of these fish would I
admit, *if possible*, into purely trout or salmon rivers,

their room being in such places far better than their
company. .There are many rivers, however, of a
mixed character, where they are found in great
abundance, and where they manage, owing to the
varied character of the water of the rivers, to do well
enough together, though even here the more delicate
fish cannot but suffer severely from them ; these
are, however, usually large rivers : in small ones, if
largely introduced and left to themselves, they would
in time almost destroy both trout and salmon. As
they *do* so exist, however, and are considered by
many as affording a wide range of sport, they must
be considered accordingly. In such cases I would
recommend artificial breeding of better fish to be
carried on largely as the only means of coping with
them.

Many rivers, again, are merely white or coarse
fish rivers, unadapted to salmon and trout ; and it is
chiefly in respect to them that I treat of them. In
rivers, however, like the Usk, Severn, and Wye,
where they have increased so much as to become
a positive nuisance, I would keep them down by
every means in my power.

Dace and roach are very fair eating when taken
in clear rivers. They may be pickled or potted or
plainly broiled, salted and peppered, a slice of butter

being laid on them while hot. Even chub can be eaten in this way, but any fish of above half a pound should be crimped. Barbel are liked well enough by some people, but the fish should be split down the back, and the backbone should be taken out before it is broiled. Indeed, few of these fish are really thrown away, for they form acceptable articles of food amongst the poorer classes, while the Jews at their various fasts employ them largely; so much so, that I have known sixteen shillings per hundred paid for average-sized dace. The Jews, however, as it is well known, are adepts in cooking fish, and we might take a useful lesson from them in this respect. Everything, however, depends as regards their toothsomeness upon the cooking. Perhaps jack and tench are the only two which are ever now subjected to plain boiling; but even with jack, veal stuffing is used to give flavour to the dish. Some people think well and some highly of jack, and formerly it was in greater request than even salmon, and it was considered a great delicacy; I cannot, of course, coincide in any such verdict. I have, however, eaten jack when it formed one of the components (scarcely an indispensable one though) of a very excellent dish, in which also were sauces and spices, wine gravy and stuffing, but the game was hardly worth the candle.

The best jack I ever ate was one of four pounds from the River Till, in Northumberland, and it certainly was an enjoyable dish; but the Till jack have a very high character, and justly. Possibly their food may have something to do with it, as no fish but the salmonidæ, minnows, and a very few perch, inhabit the Till.

Some people even yet waste port wine over carp, but sure I am that it is a mistake, at any rate, as regards our ordinary English pond carp. But I must own that we do not manage our ponds with the same care and skill that they do in Holland. Of this, however, I shall have to speak presently. In a river it cannot be denied that the carp is a far better fish than he is in a pond. Indeed, as regards its desirability both as a table and a sporting fish, its capabilities are much increased in the river. Of late years many of them have been turned into, and have escaped from private waters into the Thames; and it is found that the fish does well, increases rapidly, bites boldly, and plays very gamely; and that, too, not merely in dead dull eddies, but in the more rapid streams. There are few eddies, and a strongish stream, in the Richmond deeps; yet here three or four, from two to four or five pounds' weight, are taken almost every day throughout the season; while in the rough

and wild waters at Teddington weir, very good sport
indeed is often obtained with them, and they are
caught up to seven and eight pounds' weight. It need
hardly be observed that, in such localities, the edible
qualities of the carp are greatly improved; and so easy
a fish is it to naturalise and transport, that the only
wonder is that the Society which takes charge of the
waters of the Thames has not, with these facts
before it, introduced it more widely into all parts of
the river.

The bream is widely distributed, many of our
rivers and lakes already abounding in it. There
are two kinds: the carp bream, which is the largest
and best fish of the two; and the silver bream,
a small indifferent fish. I shall treat it more fully
when I come to ponds. In edibleness it may rank
next to the carp perhaps, and before chub and
barbel.

I come now to one or two fish which are really
rather salt than fresh water fish, though they enter
the rivers at times; and, first of all, I must notice
the little Whitebait (*Clupea alba*). All sorts of
suppositions have been made concerning this most
delicate little fish. It has been supposed to be the
fry of some score of different fish, and by slow
degrees, and careful consideration, it has proved

to be the fry of none of them, but a fish of itself.[1] The shad at one time bore away the honour of paternity from all competitors, but it was found that whitebait existed where shad did not, and shad, on the other hand, existed where whitebait had never been met with ; and as it was difficult to reconcile such apparent incongruities, the whitebait has been left to its own affiliation, and is unmolested, save by the netsmen. Some would-be-thought gourmand assert that the fry of other fish, or even minnows, if

[1] The whitebait disappears from the Thames by the middle or end of August. In the month of October I have taken it on the coast of Suffolk in almost any quantities. The variety of size amongst this fish is very remarkable, as they range of all sizes from an inch long up to seven inches, which is the largest size I have found it. At this size it somewhat resembles a small herring. Amongst the shoals were many sprats, but they could be detected at a glance. The sprats died speedily, the whitebait were much more long-lived and active. I opened one of the larger ones, but could not detect either spawn or milt, and am inclined to doubt from this whether, even when seven inches long, they are a mature fish : if they are not, then the question as to whether or no they really are a distinct species, or whether they are the fry of a yet larger fish, and if so, what that larger fish is, becomes important. I have never heard of their being taken of larger size than I have noted. Of that size Mr. Yarrel mentions them ; but he does not note whether he ever examined them for traces of their reproductive organs, with the view to proving their maturity. It certainly appears to be a migratory fish, and it would seem as if, like others of the *clupeidæ* family, its tendency in the fry state was northwards. In what form does it return thence ?

the same amount of pains were bestowed upon them,
would be equally delicious. I greatly doubt this;
nay, I utterly repudiate it, and refuse to believe it.
In matters of this especial kind I am inclined to
think that whatever is *is*. For example, turtle-soup
is, and the man who says that mock-turtle is equally
good *is* (not a judge, at any rate). The nearest thing
as a delicacy to whitebait is a dish of very small
bleak.[1] They are delicious; nay, the larger bleak,
cooked in the way that sprats are cooked, form an
excellent dish, and are scarcely inferior to gudgeon.
Having accidentally passed over the bleak, I inci-
dentally mention it here. It is a fish too well known,
though of too small importance, to need any great
space for description; and, as it is very much of a
surface-feeding fish, it takes little from the other fish,
and it affords an admirable source of food to the
more predatory fish also, as the pike, perch, and
trout; and these do feed upon it largely. The movements of a shoal of bleak on the surface of the water
are very interesting to watch; and the rapidity of
its movements, and constant restlessness, as it darts

---

[1] I should have added above, that the bleak also for a time
struggled for the honour of paternity to the whitebait, but was
soon put out of court.

hither and thither after a stray fly or floating substance, is very amusing.

As I have already said, although caught in rivers, the whitebait can hardly be called a fresh-water fish.

The Shad is a fish I have previously referred to. There are two kinds of shad. Yarrel adopts for them two names by which they were partly known before, namely, the Twaite shad and the Allice shad. The former, which used at one time to abound in the Thames (so much so that a portion of the Thames was even named Shad Thames), comes into the rivers to spawn in May, and is seldom met with after August. It is a very indifferent and comparatively worthless fish for food, being bony and coarse. Its size is from twelve to sixteen inches long.

The Allice shad is a much larger fish, running up to four or five pounds in weight. It is not so well or so commonly known as the Twaite shad. It is found more abundantly in the Severn than in any other of our rivers, and formerly afforded sport to numerous fly-fishers about Worcester, and even now many are caught. But of late years it has followed the salmon, and has greatly fallen off there. It was rarely met with in the Thames. This shad comes into the rivers to spawn, before the Twaite, usually appearing in April. For the table, it is very much the best fish

of the two. Shad may be taken both by the bait and
with the fly. The shad may be also considered as
rather more of a salt than a fresh-water fish; and as
in the case of the salmon, it is driven from the
Thames by the sewage. The higher it ascends a
river the better its flavour and condition becomes;
and, as it is a valuable and prolific fish, it should not
be neglected in any scheme for improving our fresh-
water fisheries. No doubt the Allice shad could be
introduced, by artificial breeding, to other of our
rivers, where it would be highly acceptable.

The Sturgeon occasionally enters our rivers, but it
is such a partial visitor that little is known about it
in connexion with them. The flesh is said to be
excellent, resembling veal. The great fisheries for
sturgeon are in the Caspian Sea and the rivers that
enter it, more particularly the Volga, in the Danube,
and the Baltic. It is possible that, by the transport
of ova, we might much increase the numbers of this
valuable fish in our waters, and induce it to become
a more regular visitant to the larger rivers.[1]   The

[1] The French have included the sturgeon and the sterlet in the
list of fish to be acclimatized, but the difficulties and expense of
carrying out the operation has hitherto deterred even them. I wrote
to Mons. Coume, the superintendent at Huningue, who was here in
1862 on a mission, for information as to the acclimatization of
sturgeon, but he could not give me any.

flesh is said to be excellent. Of the swimming bladder, when dried, the best isinglass is made; of the roe, the appetizing caviare is manufactured.

There is a small member of the Crustaceæ which might be cultivated far more than it is in many of our waters with great advantage. I refer to the fresh-water Crayfish.

This delicate little fish forms an excellent edible, whether eaten by itself or used for the purpose of making into soup. Crayfish soup is looked upon by gourmands, and justly, as a choice and most desirable addition to a feast. In Germany, especially, the nobles pride themselves upon their crayfish. In England, it is used, in addition to the above methods, as a garnish to turbot more particularly. In many of the rivers and streams in our midland counties, it is found in large numbers; in others, it exists, but not to an extent to make fishing for it profitable. In many tributaries of the Thames, it is very plentiful; I may instance, the Windrush, the Lambourne, and Kennet, the streams about Oxford, and in some of the smaller tributaries of the Colne. It is found, but not in abundance, in the Thames itself. The way in which it is fished for is curious. From one to two dozen small and shallow hoop nets, upon iron rings of from a foot to fifteen inches in diameter, are prepared. In

the midst of each is tied a small piece of liver. The
fisherman walks along the bank of the stream, and
drops a net thus baited into every available spot.
The iron ring carries the net to the bottom, where it
remains. Having deposited all his nets, he then
returns to the first one which he dropped in, and, by
means of a string pegged to the bank, he suddenly
hauls it up to the surface, and usually finds two or
three crayfish attracted by the liver. Having taken
them, he replaces the net in some equally desirable
spot, and goes on to the next one; returning, after an
interval, to haul them all over again. In this way,
several dozens of this little fish may be taken in a
short time.

There is little difficulty in transplanting this fish,[1]
as they can be taken when full of spawn, in June or
July, and can be carried alive to any distance, with
little trouble; and if the stream they are conveyed to
suits them, they will soon increase and multiply to
almost any extent. Rivers which are not too rapid,
and with overhanging banks and marly (not muddy)
bottoms, suit them best. They may easily be kept in
stews, but will then require regular feeding. Indeed,

---

[1] A large quantity of them have been transplanted by the Acclimatization Society of Great Britain to the Marquis of Breadal-
bane's streams.

I make no doubt but in small spaces of water, properly managed, with a sufficiency of holes and hiding-places for them, and by feeding them with fit and enough of food, they would breed and increase to any extent, and a very profitable trade carried on in them : their food need be but of small consideration, as they will eat offal in preference even to other matters.   They make good use of their nippers, when handled, and are apt to pinch somewhat sharply. One way of taking them is to thrust the hand up into the holes under old roots and banks, and letting them fasten on the fingers, to draw them out thus.   I do not strongly recommend the plan ; but the reader can try it if he likes, and, if he does not mind the pinch, will no doubt find amusement in it, particularly as he may, perhaps, occasionally lay hold of a water-rat, whose sense of his attentions will, possibly, be even more strikingly expressed.

The pearl-bearing Muscle, which abounds in many of our rivers, particularly in the Perth, in Scotland, and the Donegal river, in Ireland, might also be a subject for cultivation, as it would not only be valuable for its pearls, but form food for insects, on which the fish live in turn.   These muscles have received some little attention from the Acclimatization Society. Muscles of a somewhat similar kind are found abundantly in most of our rivers, and it is possible that some of them may even contain pearls.

The culture of Leeches is largely practised upon the Continent, and handsome profits are yearly realized by it. The best leeches come from the south of France, from Italy, and Hungary. It is doubtful whether our climate is not too cold for successful Hirudiculture. To those who wish to study this subject I recommend the work of Mons. Jourdier.

CHAPTER VII.

ON FISH TO BE ACCLIMATIZED.

At this point occurs a momentous question, viz. what fish are there which we can with advantage introduce into our rivers, that are entirely strange to them. And I shall make, perhaps, a somewhat sweeping assertion, when I aver that we have possibly too many in them already, as many of the coarser kinds being to an extent destructive to the better class of fish, we could well spare them; and beyond those I have already mentioned, there are few, if any, which it would be worth our while to introduce into our *first-class rivers*. We have already the best freshwater fish in the world in our salmonidæ; there is but one member of the salmonidæ, if we except the Coregoni, and the Northern charr, of any consequence left for us to introduce, and that is the Huchen. The huchen is said to be a very voracious fish, and among the small fry of fish particularly so. It is, moreover, of little comparative value for the table, and when much fished for it readily becomes a very shy fish to

the angler's lures.   It will only answer in our best
rivers, where we have already much better fish, which
its presence would hardly be advantageous to. Indeed,
it would take much about the same place as our own
bull-trout does, even if it were not proved to be a less
desirable fish in the long run.   For these several
reasons, I think its introduction would be a very
questionable advantage.   I would advise that we improve and increase to the utmost our salmon and
trout, and leave the huchen alone, lest we sacrifice
the substance to the shadow.

There is, perhaps, one fish mentioned by Lloyd, in his
" Scandinavian Adventures," which it might be worth
while to learn something further about, viz. the Ide.
This is a river fish ; it grows to 8lbs. or 9lbs. weight in
the Scandinavian waters, though it is not often taken
above 5lbs. or 6lbs. It is a good fish for the table, lives
chiefly upon aquatic plants and insects, and affords
good sport to the angler.   It somewhat resembles the
shad in appearance.

The Black-bass of America is another capital river
fish worth some attention.   It is excellent for the
table, and gives good sport to the angler, and in our
white fish rivers would no doubt be valuable.   It is,
however, very voracious, and some care and consideration should be exercised in acclimatizing it.   It

thrives well also in lakes, but does not object to a strong current. It is said to be a much better eating fish than the pike.

Before closing the consideration of what fish it is desirable to acclimatize, I am reminded of one which had well-nigh escaped my recollection. The Mountain-mullet of Jamaica is perhaps one of the most delicate and delicious edibles found amongst fish. In Jamaica, the estimation it is held in is so great, that a dish of mountain-mullet is the common excuse for a *recherché* dinner, and a prominent inducement to guests to partake of it; and "Dine with me, old fellow; I've a dish of mountain-mullet," seldom fails to produce the invited guests at dinner-time.

The mountain-mullet does not grow to a large size, seldom exceeding 2lbs. weight, and not often reaching that size. Inhabiting rapid rattling streams, similar to Highland burns, endued with great leaping and locomotive powers, it can make its way almost anywhere, and over any reasonable obstacle. An eye-witness assures me that he has seen one leap sheer over the huge trunk of a fallen cotton-tree, which lay like a bridge across the stream ; and although well able to hold its own in rough streams, it does well enough when these streams are shrunk to mere water-

holes by the heats of summer. But, added to its
excellent and desirable edible qualities, it presents
the strong attraction of being a capital sporting fish,
taking both fly and worm freely, and playing like a
fresh-run sea-trout when hooked. Whether the fish
would stand our winters is the question to be resolved ; in other respects, our streams would unquestionably suit it well enough. Its capabilities, also, of
being transported and acclimatized at any distance,
have also to be tested. Of its desirableness there can
be no shadow of a doubt ; and it might further be
worthy of consideration, whether, even if our winters
did not suit it, it would not be the very fish particularly suited to the fine, but fishless streams of the
Cape and many of the Australian streams, both of
which, like those of Jamaica, become rather water-
holes in summer.

CHAPTER VIII.

ON LAKES, POOLS, ETC.

An immense portion of our water acreage consists of
lakes. Such of these lakes as communicate with the
sea by means of rivers that are passable to fish are,
for the most part, capable of supporting salmon and
sea trout. In some there may be but a badly defined
passage in this respect; in these instances every art
that can render such passages practicable to fish
should be put into requisition, as a lake is always most
valuable to a river, being to the salmon a safe resting-
lace and harbour of refuge. When there are impassable falls, salmon-stairs should be erected (see
Appendix); a weir, with hatches at the outlet of the
lake, should be placed so as to force back the water,
until a sufficient quantity be collected to form a good
running volume, on the first favourable rainfall. If
salmon or sea trout exist not already in them, artificial propagation should be undertaken in the small
tributary head waters; and every possible means
should be adopted to render the salmon a tenant of its

waters. Where such communication, however, is impracticable, then the best unmigratory fish that can be introduced should be procured and encouraged.

Few lakes exist that are not favourable to the breeding or introduction of the trout, and I have already shown the best methods of proceeding with them. It will, however, be found that many small and even large lakes abound to profusion in very small trout. The smallness of these trout no doubt, in a great measure, proceeds from their being too numerous for the food found in the lakes. If the introduction of an extra amount of food, by the various means I have pointed out, be either impracticable or not thought worth the trial, the only way left is to reduce the number of trout; this can be done by netting, or by putting into the lake a certain number of jack, in order to keep the small trout down. But this last is a dangerous experiment, and, if decided on, *these jack should be* ALL MALES, in order that they may not breed, so as to increase their number; for if this be not attended to they will in time get so far ahead as almost to exterminate the trout; keeping them down will be an endless task, and they can never after be got rid of. Therefore the *greatest attention should be paid to this point.* The way to be sure on this head is to select the fish at spawning time,

when the fact can very easily be ascertained. Fish
of about a pound weight or under should be chosen;
but, under these circumstances, they should be taken
out by any possible means once every three or four
years, and replaced by others, or instead of contenting
themselves with the smaller fish they will destroy
the larger trout. As I have said before, the experiment is very hazardous, and should not be entered
upon without due consideration. But it is a well-
known fact, that all the lakes in the south of
Scotland, which produce the finest trout, have pike in
them; whether in the course of years, if the pike are
not kept down, they will continue to have trout in
them, is another matter. Long heavy nets, set as
trammels, will be found useful in such lakes, for
destroying pike.

Common trout in lakes often increase to a large
size; but there is a trout peculiar to lakes, called the
great lake-trout, or *salmo ferox*. When full grown,
the ferox is a handsome fish in appearance, but his
flesh is coarse, and, as an adjunct to the table, he is
not in very great esteem. As a matter of sport, he
is one of the strongest and gamest fish that swims
when you have hooked him;[1] and the killing of a

---

[1] As the excellent and cautious Mrs. Glasse would no doubt have
remarked if the subject of Feroxes had been brought under her
notice, "First hook your ferox."

20lb. ferox is no light triumph and no easy achieve-
ment—a 30lb. salmon is a much easier conquest.
But they rarely take anything but a trolling bait, and
that at long and weary intervals, seldom, indeed,
rising to a fly (though I have known them taken
with it). Oh, that trolling for the mythic ferox,
which has fabled itself to my mind as a species of
fresh-water kraken! How many long hours have
I spent at it bootlessly! As a destroyer of fish of
his own kind he is scarcely, if at all, less destructive
than the pike, though perhaps a more desirable fish.
These very big trout are very apt to make wastes of
the water around them. In the management of a
lake, the most useful size, if possible, to permit the
common trout to arrive at, is about 4lbs. or 5lbs.;
and with plenty of proper food in lakes, they should
not be long in arriving at that weight. After this
they grow more slowly; they feed upon their own
species more largely; and it is a question whether
they are then really worth their keep.

I treat this point here solely in a commercial view.
If I look at it as a sportsman, I should say that I
prefer a fair chance among a good show of three and
four-pounders, to that very rare one of the twelve or
twenty-pounder—one soon wearies of always sitting
in a boat, with a couple of rods stuck hopelessly

over the stern, but one seldom tires of fair sport with the fly amongst fish from 1lb. to 4lbs. or 5lbs. weight.[1] I may take occasion here to point out a singular fact, which has often been noted, but not attempted to be accounted for, and that is, that many lakes have numbers of these very large trout, running from 7lbs. or 8lbs. to 10lbs. or 12lbs. weight, and sometimes even much larger, and at the same time they have only very small fish as well. I know of many lakes where this is the case; of course, there are also many lakes where this is not so. How is it that there are so very few middle class fish, fish of 1lb. and 2lbs. or 3lbs. weight, such as the fly-fisher loves to see rising quietly and unobtrusively, just within the cast of his fly, sucking in the insects that play over and alight on the lake, as day begins to wane, and the purple shadows of the mountains begin to lengthen and deepen? Oh, for that quiet delicious hour when the cool evening breeze begins to spring up, and Nature to awake from her noontide siesta, when we can wander along the lonely strand, light of heart and freed from care, casting the seductive flies over each little circlet which betokens to the angler a goodly

---

[1] Some who may have had better success at trolling for the ferox than I or any of my friends ever had, may be disposed here to differ with me. "May difference of opinion," &c.

and a hungry trout below. Now, the cast of flies falls like thistledown, and—"by the bones of the un-canonized St. Isaac, what a head and shoulders!"—with a dash curiously unlike the way he would seize the natural fly, he has it, and turns to descend with his dangerous prize. "What, ho! bully-rook—not so fast, fair sir!" and with a slight upward turn of the wrist, the fine steel wire is fixed like the tooth of the weasel in the eagle's leg, and it shall go hard, but like it, too, it shall bring its would-be captor to land. "Hoots toots, what a pother! full twenty yards of line, as I'm a living fisherman and a sinner." That is all too far away for a near acquaintance, my dainty *salmo fario ;* so, with your leave, my scaly friend, we will gently persuade you to yield us back that twenty yards of silken web you have so lustily borrowed of us. So he feels the rankling steel, and bounds into the air like an acrobat, to see if haply he can shake it out. By this hand! three pounds if he's an ounce. Well jumped, trouty; well played, piscator. That dip of the rod-point saved your tackle *à merveille.* There's no fool at one end of the line, whatever there may be at the other. But the struggle is over at last, and poor trouty consigned to the gradually-filling creel, the prize of the evening.

"Lonely," did I say? Nay, for in yonder bay

stands knee-deep another fisherman, fishing for his evening meal too; and clever as you may be at your craft, friend piscator, Goodman Gossip Heron shall show you a trick or two of fishing which you cannot equal. How spectral and like a ghost he looks as he stands upon the watch! Ah! now you have disturbed him; he is off, and he flaps lazily away, like an over-gorged monster as he is, dropping his last capture as he goes home to Mrs. Heron and all the young Herons, who are anxiously awaiting his coming far up the face of that rugged and inaccessible rock that overhangs Loch Lonely. And now the moon begins to rise. The Lodge is two miles off across the brae; so fill thy pipe, and, with a light heart and a heavy creel, betake thee gladly and peacefully homeward, thanking God for his beautiful world and thine own happy lot in it: for *certes*, good friend, we cannot choose but envy you that fine basket of trout, that capital evening's sport, and that delicious homeward walk.

I am writing, as the reader will see, *con amore*, and I must beg him to pardon this rhapsody as an unlooked-for digression; for it is hard to be always commercially-minded on such subjects, nor ever to look at the more congenial part of the picture.

But to resume my argument. These middle-sized

L

fish are almost wanting in many lakes I could name, though small ones abound. Now, how is this to be accounted for? That the trout can easily reach the middle weight if left to themselves is proved by their reaching the greater one. May it not possibly be that these big monsters prefer the half-pounders, or fish of near that size, to their trumpery little two-ounce sons and daughters, which are far more plentiful? One thing is most certain—viz., that their capacity and capabilities are quite equal to taking even much larger fish, and they may prefer one large fish to a dozen small ones. I don't say that this *is* the reason of the absence of the intermediate size, because I cannot prove my theory, but I do think it is by no means an improbable theory. I have seen large Thames trout, of eight, ten, and twelve pounds' weight, chasing roach of half and three-quarters of a pound, and even larger ones, scores of times; and I have always found, on examining trout that have been caught, when they have had fish in them, that the fish they had chosen to devour were good-sized ones, much larger indeed than the Thames anglers usually employ as a bait. (Might not these gentlemen take a hint from this fact?)

I repeat, therefore, that, commercially speaking, up to four or five pounds should be the maximum for lake trout. Still, as others may differ from me on this point, and I do not wish to advocate my opinion too strongly, I merely record it without urging it upon anyone. But if the matter *could be* regulated as I have above put it, and it became a nice question of how many pounds of fish per annum will Loch Lonely produce me, I should be inclined to hold to my views upon the subject. Looking at the question again, as a sportsman, I care little for these big fish—these great unapproachables. They have my profound respect; should one ever chance to leave his card on me, his condescension will gratify me hugely; but the lively, free-rising two or three-pounder has my best affections, and is the object of my tenderest aspirations and hopes. Deed and truth, I'll step out in the gloaming, and scale mountains and wade bogs, like a fervent lover, to flirt with my fair young lady trout of two or three pounds' weight, when I wouldn't wet the soles of my boots for the bare chance of *seeing* her grandmother, though I should dearly like to "take a rise" out of the old lady too, if she happened to come in my way.

The angler will be rather a gainer than a loser by a proper management of the waters, and the sporting and commercial interests in all fishing matters are entirely identical. Their objects are—*the best fish,*

the best-sized fish, and the greatest number of them.
Given these three unknown quantities, what are the
relative proportions? How is this piscatorial $x\,y\,z$
to be determined? Will anyone join in trying to
work up the form of the equation? What is that
$x\,y\,z$ to be equal to? Is it to be a *plus* quantity or
a *minus* quantity? I have worked hard for many
years to make a *plus* quantity of it, and hope to be
succes ul at last. If I am, I shall not have striven
in vain—I shall have done some little good for
my fellows; for surely there is many a hungry
belly and many an empty pouch going, that might
be filled if that same equation were only properly
worked out!

The charr might certainly be much more widely
spread in our lakes than it is, if judiciously introduced.

The Ombre Chevalier, or charr of central Europe,
by some is said to be another variety. It is a very
delicious charr. Whether it really be a different
species from our charr or no, I cannot decide. Dr.
Günther holds that it is. Carl Voght gives it the
following names : " The Knight or Rotheli, Salbling,
Salmarin, Schwarzrentrel, Salmo Umbla, Salmo Salvelinus, L'Ombre Chevalier, Char," and says that it

sometimes reaches the weight of *ten pounds;* [1] and he further says, that the fish known in the lakes of Switzerland, Bavaria, and Tyrol by the names of Salbling, Salmling, Salmarin, Rothforelle, Schwarz-reuter, Alpenforelle, *are all of the same species in their variations.* Yarrel, backed by Agassiz and Nilsson, avers the identity. The breed might, however, be introduced or crossed with our own with advantage, and this could be very easily effected. As I have previously stated, some hundreds of eggs were sent to the Thames Society, who hatched them and turned them into their river. Unlike our own charr, it never leaves the lakes even to spawn, according to Dr. Günther, and, as he stated, is quite unadapted to rivers; and here is another striking point of difference from some of our charr, as in some of our lakes the charr certainly do enter the rivers to spawn.

I have not enjoyed opportunities of studying the

[1] If the Ombre Chevalier ever reaches such a weight as this, there must be some difference in the fish, as with us a charr of over 1lb. weight is a rarity, and one of 2lbs. is scarcely ever known. Dr. Günther, who has just published an interesting paper on the charr, in the proceedings of the Zoological Society, makes a strong distinction between the Umbla and Salvelinus. He says that there are at least three species in Europe not identical with our British charrs, and the British charrs are also of three different species. According to him, the Ombre Chevalier is the Salmo Umbla.

Ombre Chevalier, and must perforce accept my knowledge of it from foreign sources; yet to show how, upon matters of this nature, authorities may disagree, I may here mention the fact, that when Monsieur Coumes, the superintendent at Huningue, was a short time since in London on a mission from the French Government, he certainly stated that they were actually naturalizing this fish to the French rivers, herein greatly confirming the views which I have so often expressed with respect to the introducing of some of the charr to rivers.

Much has been written of the Lucio Perca—the pike-perch, or Sander. This, again, is a very voracious and destructive fish. It is a very fair fish for the table. It shows no sport to the angler,[1] allowing itself to be drawn from the water with scarce a struggle; and it is excessively difficult to transport, owing, apparently, to the small amount of vigorous vitality in both the fish and its eggs. M. Ekström failed in several attempts to transplant this fish from Sweden to Denmark, as the plan of artificial fecundation appears rarely to succeed, and the fish itself will not long exist when taken from the water. This is the

---

[1] I mention this point, as in acclimatizing any new fish, its capabilities, whether desirable or not, should, I think, be examined in every point of view.

account we have of it. How far modern science may be enabled to cope with the difficulty, I will not pretend to say. The French pisciculturists, however, who have much better opportunities of procuring it from Germany than we have, do not seem to have yet acclimatized it. Its voracity, however, need not be a bar to its introduction, as it is more of a lake than a river fish, and it might be placed in lakes, ponds, and such waters as are already tenanted by pike and perch, where it could do but little comparative harm, and yet be a better fish than the pike or perch. Its advent could hardly fail to be regarded favourably. I was, some time since, applied to by the Acclimatization Society to undertake the transportation of this fish from Berlin, where it is plentiful, and has a good reputation ; and, from what was stated at the time, it would have appeared that the fish there in favour was of a hardier nature than other authorities have given it credit for. I gather, however, from Herr Carl Voght's work, that there are two species of Sanders, and possibly the other, which I have not noticed, may be the fish referred to. It was not convenient to me to undertake the journey at the time, and the project was for a period laid aside.

I must now refer briefly to a class of fish found in some of our lakes, and concerning which comparatively little is known. Nevertheless, without doubt, some of them are excellent for the table. These fish are many of them but very partially distributed amongst our waters, and we have no reliable records as to how they became naturalized so partially, whether they are indigenous, or who introduced them. I refer to the class known as the Coregoni. Under this title there are some valuable members of the Salmonidæ already in some of our lakes. The Coregoni appear, for the most part, to be of little or no use to the angler, and it is therefore as regards their value for the table only that they must be altogether considered. Of those which already inhabit our own waters, there are the Powan of Loch Lomond, the Pollan of Lough Neagh, the Vendace of Loch-Maben, and the Gwyniad of Bala Lake, Llyn Tegid, and elsewhere, also called the Schelly of Ulswater.

Of all these fish, probably the Powan is the most valuable, since it grows to a fine size, from twelve to sixteen inches in length. It is called the fresh-water herring, and is excellent and wholesome food. It is abundant in Loch Lomond, and is taken in nets there in large numbers. Although it dies very soon after its removal from the water, and would thus present a difficulty towards transporting it to other lakes, still no stone should be left unturned to do so wherever the lakes are fitted for it; and artificial breeding would, no doubt, easily succeed with it.

The Pollan has sometimes been confounded with the Powan, but they are distinct fish, although the habits are very similar. The flesh, too, is rather inferior to the Powan, though not by any means to be despised. It is found chiefly in Lough Neagh, where it is in great abundance. It requires, however, to be eaten soon after its removal from the water, or it soon deteriorates. It is not quite of so large size as the Powan.

The Vendace, though found chiefly in Loch-Maben, is said not to be confined to it, as it has been stated that it is found also in other small lochs in the neighbourhood, though in smaller numbers. It seldom exceeds seven or eight inches in length. Yarrel, speaking of this fish, is satisfied that its introduction must have been effected *by means of the spawn*, as it could not be transported even a few miles alive, being of so delicate a nature. It is a very delicious fish, somewhat in flavour like to the smelt. Dr. Knox, however, speaks of it as a *moderately good fish to eat:* Dr. Knox may have eaten it under unfavourable circumstances. Of course, it is desirable that a fish so much in request as this appears to be should be more widely diffused; and I should think that, by means

of artificial breeding, it might not be difficult to
extend its range. But a judicious choice of the lake
to be stocked should be made, and I imagine that
those lakes which support its coarser and less desirable congener, the Gwyniad, might well be tried
with the Vendace. Unfortunately, it grows every year
scarcer in Loch-Maben, and it is only with difficulty
that sufficient can now be captured for the club-feasts
which are periodically held in its honour; while
casual visitors find it difficult to obtain a dish of
them.

The Gwyniad is said to be insipid and of poor
flavour, if not eaten immediately after it is caught,
and it already exists in several lakes; so that it is a
question whether it would, without some stronger
evidence of its desirability, be worth while expending
any further trouble on it. It runs to a fair size, however, nearly approaching the Powan in that respect.
There is an excellent fish of this class, called the
Fera, found in Lake Geneva. This delicious fish has
engaged the attention of French pisciculturists, who
have been largely occupied in stocking many of the
most convenient and contiguous waters of France with
it. The French Government are very liberal in trans-
mitting fecundated eggs of the Fera upon application;
and there can be little doubt but, in a few years, we

shall number this fish amongst our Fauna. There is another fish of this class, called the Lavaret, found in the Swiss lakes, which is highly spoken of for the table. It has been asserted by some that it is identical with the Fera—by others that it is also identical with the Gwyniad; but it is, I believe, now decided that it is a separate variety. Carl Voght distinguishes it from the Fera: (his description of both these fish will be found in the Appendix).

Unfortunately, the whole tribe of Coregoni are but imperfectly known, and there has hitherto existed considerable difficulty in the way of comparison. One point with regard to them is indisputable—viz., that many of them are very desirable fish to cultivate, as the food they consume is composed of insects, such as the smaller Coleoptera and the Entomostracæ. The Coregoni are said to abound in many of the American lakes, and among the most valuable is the Lake Shad, White Fish, or *Coregonus Albus.* The following is a description of this fish, from Mr. Hunter's work on the Scenery, &c. of the Eastern Townships of Canada:—" Form oval, slightly tapering towards the tail; body deep and thick; head pointed, and with the *mouth very small;* average weight about four pounds. Colour silvery, bluish-grey on the back; lighter on the sides, and pearly-white on the belly. This is a most excellent fish, and nearly all are disposed to acquiesce in this opinion. It is taken in considerable numbers in Lake Massawippi, and in the other lakes of the Eastern Townships." This would evidently be a very desirable fish for our waters, and, no doubt, would suit most of our lakes.

In the Appendix, appended to and connected with this subject, will be found a note from Dr. Günther, to whom I had written with respect to the Coregoni, and the reader will see that he quite confirms all that I have said regarding them, and the difficulty and confusion existing.

There are many American fish recommended strongly by various authorities as useful for our waters. I have already alluded to the Black Bass in treating of rivers. This fish is also suitable for lakes, where it might be really useful, and there could not be much difficulty in obtaining it.

The great Maskinongé rather resembles the pike in appearance. It inhabits the large lakes in Western Canada chiefly. This fish has been known to reach 70 lbs. and even 80 lbs. in weight. That which I have said concerning the voracity of the black bass, applies more forcibly here ; and I may remark that it is a question if we do not already possess, in the pike and the perch, two fish equally good with the above-

named fish; and it would be worth while to consider, whether it be advisable to increase the number
of destructive and voracious fish which inhabit our
waters, and which might by any accident become
naturalized in our more valuable fisheries, where their
introduction would be but a nuisance and a mis-
fortune. If, however, variety be thought desirable,
where it can do no harm, I have nothing further to
urge against it.

The Silurus (*Silurus Glanis*) is a fish of very
singular habits. It exists in many of the Swedish
lakes—formerly it abounded in Denmark. It is
found to grow to a very large size in the Danube,
even up to the weight of 300 lbs. It is, therefore,
alike a lake and river fish. The flesh is said to be
very excellent for the table. The habits of the fish
are sluggish, but it is amazingly voracious, and, such
being the case, we might well hesitate to introduce a
fish which has the capability of increasing to 300 lbs.
weight, and the capacity for creating a watery desert
around him. Not being active in its movements, it
has recourse to cunning, and takes its victims after
the same fashion as the " angler or fishing-frog." By
means of plying the barbels on its nose, it attracts
the fish, and they are immediately engulphed in the
huge cavernous mouth, which rises from below, where

the fish lies perdue—its concealment being much
aided by the colour of its body, which resembles the
soil that surrounds it. It is a fish much resembling
the burbot, both in shape and habits, hiding itself in
holes, or under roots or tree-stumps. It is very
tenacious of life, and therefore, if it were thought
desirable to transport it, there would not be much
difficulty in the attempt. Our Norfolk meres, and
such sheets of water, might be advantageously used
possibly for it. I may add that it has been known
to devour an infant entire, and even the body of a
woman has not proved too large an obstacle to the
voracity of one of unusual size.

CHAPTER IX.

ON SMALLER PONDS.

I now come to ponds; and here, perhaps, we display our very worst management. The Dutch, by judicious treatment of their resources in this respect, realize large revenues, and produce fish which are really said to be palatable, and even excellent. But what is the English pond-fish worth? In ninety cases out of a hundred, the flavour of mud is so painfully evident, that for any table purposes the fish is worthless. In fact, by putting fish into our ponds, we simply spoil them. Take a carp, for example, from a river, and he is, as I have said, perhaps, a fairly eatable fish. Take him from one of our ponds, and few will care to eat him. Why is this? It is because we do not study how best to keep our ponds in good order— clean, sweet, and wholesome.

In the first place, we, for the sake of picturesqueness, and to add to the beauty of the landscape, plant trees all round our ponds, or to a certain extent round them. These trees yearly shed their

leaves : the surface of the ponds may, in the autumn,
be seen covered with them. The leaves become
saturated with water and sink to the bottom of the
pond, where they accumulate into a perfect bed, or
thick layers of leaves. These, acted on by the water,
slowly decompose, the action continuing for months,
until they gradually turn into thick, black, and
stinking mud. During the decomposition of these
leaves, and also after their decomposition, they continue to send forth noisome gases and exhalations,
which penetrate and pervade the water, from which
an unwholesome mist and smell ascends, more or
less at all times, and particularly in hot moist
weather. Under these circumstances, how is it possible that the fish inhabiting these waters so affected
should be otherwise than receptacles for a species of
concentrated essence of mud? To add to the effect,
we leave our ponds year after year without cleaning them out, and the weeds grow and rot. and grow
and rot year after year, and, combined with the leaves
from above, the pond literally grows mud, until at
length the ponds either so fill up or become such a
nuisance that they generate deadly diseases, and necessitate a heavy and expensive operation for the carting
away of the almost liquid filth thus formed. Ponds
cannot be kept too clean, and no more weed should

be permitted to accumulate in them than is just
sufficient for shelter, and the production of food for
the fish. In Holland, where, as I have stated, this
subject is properly studied and understood, the ponds
are usually made in series or chains of two, three, or
more, communicating by hatches with one another;
so that when one is drained the others may remain
full, and each or all of them can be raised or let down
at pleasure. One or the other of them is usually
drained down and left dry yearly, or every year or
two, for some months, in order to allow the soil to
exhale and the weeds to die down. Some weeds
are indispensable, as they harbour food, and are more
particularly needed for the fish to spawn amongst.
Indeed, the fish cannot spawn without them; and,
added to this, the spawn is said to require the aera-
tion afforded by the weeds for its proper vivification.
The little gold fish often die off in great numbers,
from no other cause than that of being placed in
tanks or reservoirs where there are no weeds for it
to rub itself against, in order to free itself from the
spawn. The Water Crowsfoot is one of the most
useful weeds for ponds, but the Alsinastrum should
be avoided, or it will soon choke up the pond.

Ponds should be fished once in every three or four
years; they do not pay if left for longer intervals.

M

A few pairs of the larger fish should be left as breeders, with whatever fry may exist; but the middle-sized fish should be taken out—that is, the fish from two to four or five pounds. Carp, for example, grow slowly up to about three-quarters of a pound weight, when they seem to strike out and grow very rapidly up to five or six pounds, if food be plentiful and the water of good temperature. From this onwards they grow again much more slowly, and the fish take up, when large, more space than they are worth; for these large carp are also unmarketable, the fish from two to five pounds being best for the table, the large ones being apt to get woolly and tasteless.

Mr. Simeon, in his most able and interesting work, "Stray Notes on Fishing, &c.," gives a very good account of the operations of Mr. Maltby, our Vice-Consul at Brussels, who has several ponds in that locality for the rearing of fish. From this account valuable data may be derived. Mr. Maltby, it seems, does not rely altogether upon his own breed of fish, but buys others of the best and most approved breeds, to introduce from time to time into his waters, thus crossing the breeds. According to Mr. Simeon, Mr. Maltby finds the Tench perhaps the most valuable pond-fish of any, being the most delicate and free from any muddy flavour; and in this estimate I

think my own experience verifies his, as I have eaten
Dr. Tench, as he is sometimes called, even from *our*
ponds with a reasonable amount of satisfaction.

After the formation of a pond, it is often found
that the fish do not thrive nor increase. There
may be various reasons for this: one is that, possibly, the soil of the pond does not suit the fish
nor encourage food for them; a soft, warm, marly
bottom being the best. Gravel (often impregnated
with iron) does not do well, nor does a hard clay,
which is too cold and unproductive. Again, steep
banks with deep water all around the sides are
objectionable, as the fish like to push on to the
shallows, and lie with their backs almost above
water, both for spawning and for warmth; and besides this, the small fry, when just hatched and
capable of moving about, cannot exist in the deep
water, but require shallows as an absolute necessity.
This will be recognised either in rivers or ponds, if
the reader will remember, when he has been walking
along the banks at certain seasons, how often he has
seen the small fry start off from the margin, where
they have been sunning and disporting themselves
in myriads, and how seldom, on the other hand, he
has ever noticed them in deep water. Ponds that
have rookeries besides them have been found not

to answer. The reason of this is that the droppings of the rooks, which are very considerable, contain a large percentage of lime, which is very prejudical to fish.

The best fish for ponds are Carp, Tench, Jack, and Bream. It is always well, even in carp and tench ponds, to have a few brace of jack among the carp and tench, for the purpose of keeping the fry down, so that they may not devour too much of the food from the larger fish. The proportions recommended by Mr. Boccius, who is an authority upon this subject, having written a work upon it, are 200 brood carp, twenty brood tench, and twenty brood jack to the acre, the best time of stocking being the end of October; and this, as he points out, is a matter of some importance.

With regard to the growth of Pike, I have been much astonished, in looking over Mr. Simeon's work, to find the following remarkable statement, which I give literatim. It will be seen, that a good and constant supply of fresh water, and that of as warm a temperature as may be reasonably gained, are very favourable matters to the growth of fish. He is speaking of Mr. Maltby's undertaking :—

"Although both lakes, La Hulpe and Boilsfut, are fairly well supplied by springs and natural streams, yet he believes the qualities of the waters flowing through them to be different, the sources from which they are derived being distinct.

" With a view, therefore, of promoting the growth of his fish—a change of water being in his opinion the means which, more than any other, conduce to improve both their size and quality—he every other year transports the smaller fish from Boilsfut to La Hulpe, and *vice versa*. This he effects by carting them across in barrels, the proportion of water to fish in each being one-third water and two-thirds fish. In order to insure them a due supply of air during the transit, the hole in the side of each barrel is bunged up with a wisp of straw. By the jolting of the cart the fish are kept in continual motion, and, while the water is prevented from escaping, it becomes, by being shaken against the straw, sufficiently charged with external air for the purpose of respiration. By adopting this mode of carriage, he never loses five pounds' weight out of three thousand pounds transported.

" The effect which such a change has upon jack appears to be most remarkable, the increase in their weight, after removal, being, in some cases, at the rate of not less than from *eight to ten pounds a year*. In the year 1856, for instance, Mr. Maltby marked and

transferred from the large lake of Boilsfut to that of
La Hulpe, forty-five jack, averaging one with another
two pounds each; none of them weighing more than
three pounds. In eighteen months from the time
when they had been thus transferred, many of these
same fish were caught by trolling, having attained
the weight of from fifteen to twenty pounds, being at
the extraordinary rate above mentioned.

"This increase in the size of the jack was so sudden and unexpected, that nearly all the smaller fish
were destroyed by them, before any steps could be
taken for their removal. It was, however, then effected
by letting out the water, when the jack were placed
in one of the smaller ponds above mentioned. In
this however, although it contained a good supply of
white fish, they rather lost than gained weight, probably, as Mr. Maltby imagines, in consequence of
there being a smaller body of water running through
it, and that colder, from being nearer the source.

"At the commencement of the year 1857, he had
purchased and turned into the lake at Boilsfut nine
hundred carp of a particularly good breed, weighing,
one with another, a pound each; but of these, when
the water was let out in the month of October, not a
single one was to be found, the jack not having
suffered a solitary individual to escape them. Since

that time Mr. Maltby has allowed no jack to be put
into his water, as stock, above a pound in weight,
which (as younger fish do not gain weight so fast,)
will not increase in a year to more than about three
or four pounds. It is only after attaining that weight
that their growth becomes so astonishingly rapid.

"In the lake at Boilsfut, jack, perch, and white
fish breed fast, but the fish born in that lake do not
increase so fast by two-thirds as those born in La
Hulpe; so that, although their transport from the
one to the other is expensive, yet it is made up for by
the increase of weight in the fish transported."

These facts are both interesting and astonishing,
and are well worthy the attention of pisciculturists.
We have no record of jack growing at such a rate in
this country, and I believe the case is rather excep-
tional.

Roach, save as food for the jack, are worse than
useless in ponds, and should never be introduced
where there are carp, or they will in time exterminate
the carp: the roach increase so rapidly, and are so
much more active than the carp, that they will in
time literally starve the carp. I have had occasion to
note this on more than one occasion. I will instance
one. In Brownwich Pond, near Titchfield, in Hampshire (a pond formerly belonging to a monastic insti-

tution), there were, when I was a boy, a great abundance of very fair sized carp ; there were also a quantity of roach, running up to a quarter and half a
pound in weight: there were plenty of eels, and a
tolerable proportion of trout.   Of the latter I usually
got from two to half a dozen in the course of my
day's fishing ; they rarely, however, exceeded half a
pound in weight.   The carp did not run large, owing,
as I believe, to the numerous roach, four or five
pounds being the largest I ever saw there.   Fish of
from one to two or two-and-a-half pounds were plentiful, and I could usually, with a float and worm, take
from twenty to thirty or forty pounds' weight in a day.

I had not visited this pond for many years, when,
happening to be in the neighbourhood some time
since, I resolved again to fish it with a friend.
The trout, I was informed, had entirely disappeared
for some time.   The pond was literally alive with
small roach.   Any person standing in one spot
could easily, with one fragment of worm, and without ever changing his bait, take three or four
dozen of them, provided, and as long as, any worm
was left on the hook, and it mattered very little
what spot he selected.   Our whole day's fishing
produced us hundreds (I cannot say how many) of
these wretched little roach, some half-dozen small

eels (much smaller than formerly), and three carp, the largest about three-quarters of a pound, and all three of them so starved and so wretchedly thin that, as my friend remarked, one might almost shave oneself with their backbones—the length and head being those of two-pound fish if in fair condition. I should think that one or two more years would certainly, if no remedial measures were adopted, see the last of the carp. The roach themselves, too, had diminished to the smallest size, being not larger than bleak, say fifteen or twenty to the pound.

Eels, again, are bad things to have in a pond, as the destruction they work among the spawn is very great; and if the reader cares for his fish, let him by no means be tempted to indulge in the picturesque, by placing swans or ducks or fancy waterfowl of any kind on his pond: if he does, he will certainly maintain them at the expense of the fish. If he must have a pair of swans to look pretty, let him get a skilful taxidermist to stuff him a pair as life-like as possible; he may even, to render the illusion more real, put some clockwork into them, to make them nod their heads every five minutes; let him then anchor them far out in the middle of his pond, and for all picturesque purposes his end will be answered. Knowing the mischief they do, I detest swans, and wish evey swan was, like his sable brother, a "*rara avis in terris*," or rather *aquis*. One had better throw open his pond or river to all the poachers in the district than indulge in a taste for swans. If any one doubts this, let him take a row up the Thames from Weybridge to Chertsey, or on to Laleham, during the latter end of the month of April or early in May, and take particular and especial notice of what the swans are doing. If he has still any doubt, and likes to kill one or two and cut them open, he will solve his doubts and do a service at the same time : he may be fined for it, but he will certainly suffer for a good action and in a good cause. A swan can and will devour a gallon of fish-spawn every day while the spawn remains unhatched, if he can get it, and it is easily found. I leave the reader to calculate what the few hundreds (I might almost say thousands) on the Thames devour in the course of two or three months. Their greediness and voracity for fish-spawn must be witnessed to be believed. If this were not so, the Thames ought to swarm to excess with fish, whereas it is but poorly supplied.[1]

[1] Here is a little calculation. Suppose each swan only to take a quart of spawn per diem, which is a very low average indeed ; suppose each quart to contain 50,000 eggs (not a tithe of what it does contain)—I am not speaking of salmon or trout here, their ova

To these facts some will probably demur, and use a common argument, that "*They* never saw the swans eat fish-spawn, although they have seen swans at feed hundreds of times." This is very probable. Gentlemen usually go on the water, and take particular note of things appertaining to the water, during the pleasant warm months of the year, when fish do not spawn, and therefore, of course, they see nothing of this. Besides, such an argument, if it be argument, is nothing in the face of facts. I have seen them, and I know very many other people who have. The late Mr. Arthur Smith and Mr. Frank Buckland were appointed, by the Thames Society, to try and mitigate the swans. They went up the river some miles, for the sole purpose of assuring themselves of the facts first, never having previously actually noticed them; and they came back thoroughly convinced of all that I have stated, from ocular demonstration. Many, many times I have

being much larger; suppose only 200 swans (about a fourth, perhaps, of the number really employed) are at work at the spawn, and give them only a fortnight for the period of their ravages. Now, what is the result we get? Why, a little total of 140,000,000. One hundred and forty millions of eggs! Suppose only half of those eggs to become fish, and we have a loss of seventy millions of fish every year to the River Thames—a heavy price to pay for the picturesque, particularly when the reality may perhaps be doubled, or trebled, or even quadrupled.

striven to drive the swans away from their disgusting
meal, and with very little success. They will suffer
you when thus engaged to come near enough to
strike them with a stick—nay, they will almost fight
for the spawn, and the moment your back is turned
they commence anew. I dwell upon this point with
special force, because all poaching and all other means
of destruction sink into utter insignificance beside the
ravages of swans, particularly on the Thames.

I once, when at Marlow early in the month
of May, saw the long shallow some distance below
the river covered with large fish (barbel, chub,
roach, &c.) engaged in depositing their spawn. I
watched them for some days; how long they had
been there before I came I know not. The shallow,
for near a hundred square yards, was black with
shoals of fish; so thick were they in places that I, who
happened one day to be fly-fishing, could not throw
the fly on the water in many parts without foul-hook-
ing either a large roach or a chub. At length the fish
ceased spawning, and dropped off the shallows, exhausted, into the deeper, stiller water below. As
soon as the fish left, I saw a troop of swans, about
five-and-twenty in number, come sailing up the
river, led by a patriarchal old villain with a huge
knob over his beak. He appeared perfectly aware of

what he was going about, for he led his band direct
to the shallow, and immediately the whole troop
commenced ripping up the spawning beds, and devouring the spawn. In spite of all my efforts to drive
them away, I could never manage to keep them off
the beds for more than two or three minutes at a
time. By hook or by crook, they would manage to
get upon some part of the bed, and repeat the rip-
ping-up and gorging process. For ten days those
twenty-five swans gorged themselves to repletion,
night and day, upon the spawning beds; and I
believe they must have devoured in that time a
small barge-load of spawn. Two men, engaged night
and day, could hardly have kept them off the bed.
I pointed this out again and again to the fishermen
about there, but they seemed not to care about it.
How much longer these devouring brutes stayed on the
beds I know not, for I was obliged to leave the place
before they had finished their feast; but that almost
the whole yearly produce of the river for miles below
was then and there devoured by the swans, I have
not a particle of doubt, as there are no shallows fit for
spawning for a considerable distance below that spot.

But to return to Pond-fish. Perch thrive fairly in
some ponds, but not in others, as they rapidly get the
muddy flavour so common to English pond-fish. Many

of the small lakes in the south of Scotland abound
with them, and in some of the lakes they seem to do
well, often being taken of three and four pounds in
weight.   For marketable and table purposes a perch
of from half a pound to a pound is to be preferred.
If ponds are fit for trout, having a good stream into
them, I would put no other fish whatever in with them.

Mr. Boccius, in his work upon Pond-fish, recommends a species of carp found in Holland,
called the Spiegel, or Mirror carp.   He avers that
it is as far superior to the ordinary carp for table
purposes, as it excels it in beauty of appearance.   A
curious feature worth noting in this Spiegel carp
is a row of very large scales of various sizes, along
the side, which are of a mottled blue colour.   It
appears at times to grow to a very large size.

Gudgeon, as I have before stated, will do well in
ponds, and may advantageously be introduced into
them.

I now come to the Pike, and little more can be said
of him, as already he is in many instances an intruder
and too widely spread, and monopolises many waters
which formerly were full of fine trout.   In some lakes,
as I have before said, he is for a time useful, and
the trout increase in size ; but the breed of pike in
these lakes, if they have managed to establish a breed,

should be kept down by every possible means, and the larger fish, particularly, sought out and killed by any device that can be employed, or in a few years the nice trout-lake will become a pike pond. The best time to thin them out is at spawning time, when a net, placed quietly round the shallow parts of the lake, where weed and reed beds are, will secure any quantity of the stock of the lake. The big ones can then be taken out, and killed if not wanted, or sent off to regular pike waters, where they will be welcome, and the remaining stock regulated. For this purpose the fisherman should commence his operations in the early part or middle of April.

In many of the lakes which salmon frequent, the pike is a most destructive pest, as the time when the salmon-smolts are passing down to the sea is a regular jubilee with them, and myriads of fish ten times more valuable than themselves are devoured by them. Here they should be exterminated: it should be " *Guerra al Trimmer-o!* "—"War to the Trimmer" even.[1] In many of the ponds, canals, and reservoirs of the midland counties, on the other hand, his presence is most welcome; and as he already inhabits most of these localities, little can be done for him but to treat him fairly, and fish with moderation. The

---

[1] Not excepting spear, spade, spud, or anything else whatever.

best pike I ever saw, if I except the Till fish already
mentioned, are, without question, the Trent pike, both
for shape and make and for the table. They are
short, thick, well-fed, handsome fish, with firm white
flesh, and every other good quality which can belong
to a pike. In ponds pike are less liable to the muddy
flavour than the other fish : how this is I know not. I
have tasted carp from a pond of very muddy flavour,
and jack from the same pond almost destitute of it ;
so that is a point in his favour. A jack, of from one
to three or four pounds' weight, may be *made* very fair
eating, as I have before stated. To the sportsman he
is welcome, as coming at a time when salmon and
trout are out of season, and altogether the pike is not
a bad fish *in his place :* out of it he is a perfect pest.

Of Bream, there are two kinds, the white and the
carp bream. The white bream is comparatively
worthless, both for the table and the sportsman, as it
is of small size and bad flavour. The carp bream
grows at times to a very large size in the Irish
lakes, where a bream fisherman would be satiated
with the sport, as cartloads are often caught at one
drag of the net.[1] They are sometimes taken up to

[1] In Lough Erne vast shoals of bream may occasionally be seen
swimming at the surface and rippling the water, so as to resemble
the effects of a sudden puff from a breeze of wind.

to ten and twelve pounds' weight. They will do well
in a pond with carp and tench, particularly if there are
any deep holes in it, and they will afford variety for
the sportsman; but they are of no great value for the
table, as I think, probably, split and dried like had-
docks is the best way of preparing them. They are
salted and eaten largely by the poor in Ireland. The
French have an old motto, to the effect that "he who
hath bream in his pond may bid his friends welcome."
There is no accounting for taste.

Note.—All knowledge is progressive, and in a new science like
pisciculture new facts are elicited from week to week, and from
month to month; and I may here, before closing the subject of
lakes and ponds, take occasion to state the results of two or three
experiments which have just come to light, tending to show that
young salmon can and will exist in lakes or ponds for years without ever going to the sea. Some experiments show that they will
grow up to 3lbs. and 4lbs. weight, but that they do not get into
good condition, being white and flabby in flesh, and that they
usually die off when they reach that size. Other experiments
apparently show that they do not grow to so large a size, but keep
their condition much better than is above stated. Probably this
may turn out to be merely a matter of feeding. The fact, however,
that salmon-fry can exist for years without going to the sea, seems
to be tolerably certain, and is by no means a valueless one; and
I have thought it desirable to mention it here, although it is somewhat out of place, rather than omit it altogether.

CHAPTER X.

OUR SEA FISHERIES.

IF our ignorance of the value of our inland fisheries is to be deplored, assuredly the ignorance which exists upon a matter so vital to us as our sea fisheries is ten times more deplorable. Situated as England is, where would she so naturally turn for a constant and unfailing supply of hardy sailors, in case of a great naval war, as to our fisheries? The importance of these aids to our naval power has always been clearly recognised until of late years. Formerly, so great a store was set by this source of supply, that the Government granted bounties in respect to the fish taken in our herring fisheries; and there can be no question that the system, in a national point of view, was a wise one, and worked well, and that the withdrawal of it has had an injurious effect upon this source of manning the navy.[1] Even as a matter of

---

[1] Strangely enough, just as we have given up the system of bounties, France—who is straining every nerve to create a great navy—has taken it up.

pounds, shillings, and pence, I cannot but think the country was a gainer by it. In the first place, it induced a very large number of families to follow the business, and so fostered an important branch of industry. It threw a much larger supply of fish into the markets, and created exports instead of imports, as I shall take occasion to point out presently. It caused large numbers of our fishermen to occupy grounds now occupied for the most part by foreign fishermen, who thus improve their naval resources at the expense of ours. And lastly, but not leastly, it caused a great number of lads to be trained to the sea, and to become the best and hardiest of sailors, at no further expense to the country; whereas we have now to keep training-ships and training-schools, at a vast expense to the country, and propositions are made for a naval militia. The lads so trained being, for the most part, landsmen, instead of used to the sea from their cradles, while in such a fair-water, smooth-sailing way of making sailors, it is impossible but what an inferior article must be turned out, to the handy, hard-a-weather set of men, who keep the sea in all weathers, for eight or nine months in the year, in small craft, by dint of sheer seamanship. Now, put training ships and schools in the one scale, and the bounty in the other; consider carefully the materials produced by the two, and I

think I may venture to reassert, that the system of
bounties was a wise and, for us, a necessary one.

So little is the subject of our sea fisheries thought of
or understood, that, save the persons actually engaged
in them, no one knows or cares anything about it.
Where the haddock comes from, which the modern
Briton eats for his breakfast; or whence the cod, that
aids his Christmas dinner; or how the salt-fish is taken,
which he keeps fast on in Lent : he knows and cares
no more than he does to know whether there be fish
or no in the rivers of the moon—possibly not so
much. Yet is fish an article, not only of daily consumption, but almost hourly consumption : we eat it
at every meal. For are not shrimps and prawns, and
even at times the domestic bloater, ornaments of the
tea-table?—while who has not eaten pickled salmon
for supper, yea, though the penalty be nightmare?
This indifference can proceed from nothing but very
general ignorance, and this ignorance makes the
subject a difficult one to handle. Authorities, whence
one may draw inspiration and wisdom, are fully as
scarce as our knowledge. Fortunately, there are one
or two gentlemen of knowledge and scientific attain-
ments whom I can quote upon this subject; for the
knowledge of the fishermen themselves is so beset
with prejudice and inconclusiveness, that it would

be worse than useless for my purpose. Mr. William Andrews, the President of the Natural History Society of Dublin, has written a good deal upon this subject, and has written it well, and with much and valuable experience.

Formerly, one of our most valuable fisheries was the Newfoundland Fishery. The quantities of cod and ling which we got thence were enormous, while the Banks formed the best school for sailors we had. Let us see what Mr. Andrews has to say about Newfoundland. Quoting from a paper read by him before the Royal Society of Dublin, I find the following. Speaking to the same effect that I have, of the importance of our fisheries, as a school and training-ground for sailors, he says :—

"In 1663, a document was issued by Charles the First, and directed to the Lord Treasurer and others, desiring them 'to erect a common fishery for the nursery of seamen, which contained the first regulations for the governing of his Majesty's subjects inhabiting in Newfoundland, and trafficking in bays ;' but from the earliest periods the policies pursued by the Government, especially the Board of Trade, tended much to weaken the position of the original settlers there, and to damp their energy and perseverance in extending the fisheries. The Act, however, of 10th and 11th of William and Mary, declares the fisheries of Newfoundland a beneficial trade to the kingdom, in the employment of a great number of seamen and ships, by the increase of her Majesty's revenue, and the encouragement of trade and navigation. The same parliament came to a resolution, 'That the fisheries and trade of Newfoundland do very much promote navigation, increase seamen, and are of great profit to the nation.'

"In the reign of Elizabeth, there were 260 ships employed in the Newfoundland fisheries, and the seamen nursed in these fisheries mainly assisted in manning her fleets. Act 15th, George III. 'declares the fisheries the best nurseries for able and experienced seamen, always ready to man the royal navy when occasion may require; and it is of the greatest national importance to give all due encouragement to said fisheries.' In fact, from the British fisheries, Britain derived the principal means of defending herself; for it had been remarked that neglect and want of proper encouragement to our fisheries would much affect our commercial marine, and consequently our naval ascendancy.

"The French saw these advantages to the naval power of Great Britain, and therefore, by every influence and exertion, endeavoured to obtain equal position and benefit. The French, therefore, spared no encouragement to stimulate their fisheries, gave bounties on the fish exported from Newfoundland, or from France to the French colonies. Bounties were also allowed on all men and boys sailing annually from France, and that were employed in the shore and bank fisheries of Newfoundland. On the other hand, so discouraging had been the countenance of the Government to the British fisheries, that the capitals embarked in them were by degrees withdrawn, and the nurseries of seamen, so justly valued, almost entirely lost. They still more rapidly declined after the treaties of 1814 and 1818, when the greater and the most valuable parts of the Newfoundland fisheries were ceded to the French. The Americans zealously followed the example of France, supported their fisheries by bounties and other encouragements, and thus, concurrently with the French, sapped the foundation of the British fishery. The British fishermen, being unable to contend with the unequal competition, were left to languish and to deteriorate, being chiefly employed in the in-shore fisheries in small craft; while the French and the Americans prosecuted with vigour the deep-sea fishing on the great Banks of Newfoundland—these Powers, it is stated, employing at least 1,000 vessels of considerable burthen. and manned with not less than 30,000 seamen.

" The valuable report, dated 2d October, 1848, addressed to the Vice-Admiral, the Earl of Dundonald, by Captain Granville G. Loch, R. N., upon the fisheries of Newfoundland and Labrador, when in command of her Majesty's ship *Alarm* (an ominous name), conveys most forcibly the state of the British fisheries, in comparison with the advantages possessed and maintained by the French. Captain Loch heard the French speak with pride of the sailors their bankers produced, and of the hardships and dangers they were exposed to in fishing on the banks, and that to deprive their country of these fisheries would be to lop off the right arm of her maritime strength."

To the above notice of the fisheries I will add a few facts. In 1517, the first English vessel that visited the coast of Newfoundland, found French, Spanish, and Portuguese engaged in the traffic. In 1615, England had 200 ships there, while the French, Biscayans, and Portuguese had 400. Many of these ships carried twenty guns, eighteen boats, and from ninety to a hundred men. In the early part of last century, the inhabitants of New England had about 1,200 tons of shipping employed in the whale-fishery; and, with their vessels engaged in the cod-fishery, they

caught upwards of 23,000 quintals of fish, worth 12s.
per quintal, which they exported to Spain and the
Mediterranean, and remitted the proceeds in payment
for English manufactures. In 1745, the annual value
of the North American fisheries was stated to be
982,000l., or close upon a million a year; and this, of
course, represents a far larger value in the present
time than it did a hundred years ago. In 1787, the
number of British vessels engaged was 402, employing 16,856 men, while, besides large quantities
of fish, there were nearly 2,400 tons of oil exported.
In 1814, the exports of fish and oil amounted to
nearly 3,000,000l. The advantage to this country,
nationally, may be summed up in the words of
De Witt : " That the English navy became formidable
by the discovery of the inexpressibly rich fishery-
ground of Newfoundland."

Now let us see what our paternal Government
has been doing with this most valuable possession—
3,000,000l. a year, and the men for a fleet. The richest
gold-mines in our possession cannot equal this, for
they are exhaustible : properly worked, Newfoundland is inexhaustible. In 1857, a treaty was con-
cluded between our Government and France, in which
the British Government literally handed over the
most valuable part of the Newfoundland fisheries to

the French, granting to them the *exclusive right* of occupying large tracts on the coast, for the purpose of cleaning, packing, &c., with other rights of a judicial and imperial nature. Now this treaty was at first a secret treaty, entered on without even the knowledge of the parties most concerned—the Nova Scotians themselves; and to give the treaty an air of fairness, a proviso was inserted in it to the effect, that if the treaty were refused by the Government of Nova Scotia, it should be void and of no effect. When the treaty became known to the inhabitants of Newfoundland, meetings were held, and great indignation expressed, as a matter of course. The treaty was indignantly repudiated by the Government, and delegates were appointed to proceed to England, and bring their case before Parliament. Upon hearing this, *Mr. Labouchere assured them, that as they repudiated the treaty it could not take place, and was therefore at an end.* The deputies consequently, relying upon the word of a member of the Government, did not prosecute their intention, but remained at home. Nevertheless, in spite of this, the French fishermen and authorities proceeded to act upon it, and riots and serious outbreaks occurred at St. John's; and when our Government was applied to for information, either the information was refused, or it was asserted that as the Nova Scotians refused the treaty, it did not exist. Still the French proceeded to act upon it, and gave a threatening notice to the inhabitants of St. George's Bay to quit their rights, and to cease to use the shores as they had always been accustomed to—a notice equivalent to confiscating their property. The President of the Chamber of Commerce then wrote to the British Commandant on that station, Sir Houston Stewart, complaining of these encroachments, and he replied, that "The interpretation of treaties must be left to the Imperial Government;" and consequently, although the treaty is *legally* void, according to the terms of it, it is acted upon by the French, and our Government do not seek to prevent it.

It may be urged that a work of this nature is hardly the right place to rake up treaties and matters of Government; but if these things affect the wellbeing or cause the depression of our fisheries, I would ask— how is it possible to consider how our fisheries may be improved, and yet to ignore the chief causes of their failure? I know that these subjects are not popular studies, and that the merest *ad captandum* account is too often accepted by Englishmen, instead of a searching inquiry into the facts being exercised; and it is owing to such carelessness that bad laws or treaties, injurious to our interests, are made and suffered to pass unquestioned, or, at least, unaltered when they are made : consequently, as I have said, it is very much from the bad laws made by Government, or the want of that protection which they should receive from the Government, that the unsatisfactory state of our fisheries for the most part proceeds.

In speaking further of the depression of the Irish fisheries, Mr. Andrews says that the quantity of salt-fish imported into Ireland yearly amounts to 1,200 tons, valued at 27,000*l.*; the annual import of her-rings at about 80,000 barrels, valued at 128,000*l.* ; and this, too, at a time when the fisheries around the Irish coasts are not only far more than equal to any demand that can be made upon them, but, properly worked, would also be inexhaustible. Mr. Andrews, in his voyages from port to port and place to place in pursuit of knowledge on fishery matters, frequently mentions the fact of seeing immense shoals of pil-chards and herrings weeks before they could be attempted to be taken by the fishermen, owing to the fact of the smallness of their boats and insufficiency of their gear. He mentions other cases of foreign craft loading with fine fish off the coast in a few days, and sailing for their respective ports ; while there was not a craft on the coast that could come into competition with them, and the natives could but look on while the foreigner filled his pockets with what should have been their wealth, if they only possessed the means to take it. This, as Mr. Andrews points out, is from the poverty of the inhabitants and *the absence of encouragement.*[1] I will again quote from his excellent paper :—

"The men of Skerries and of Rush, who once followed annually the deep-sea fishery (and when the bounty was given, large quantities of ling and cod were brought home and cured at Rush), still inherit the desire to make their north-west cruises. In 1853 this spirit stimulated them to fit out four vessels for Iceland ; but not having good information when on the grounds, and being late in arriving there, they were not successful. French vessels had made good their fishing before the Skerries boats were prepared. In 1855, three vessels were again fitted at Skerries, averaging fifty tons each, with a crew of eight men and a boy. The vessels had equal success. The first that returned had 21,000 cod, with a large quantity of oil. The weather on the fishing-grounds was changeable and foggy, with heavy swells. They left

[1] With our existence depending on our resources as a naval power, and, *if possible, upon our exclusive possession of those resources,* surely it is nothing very outrageous to ask that some means of encouraging the prosecution of these valuable fisheries should be found ?

in April, and were twenty-one days going out; and
returned in August, nine days coming home. If the
weather had been favourable in the commencement,
they might have completed their cargoes in two
months. This is the way to make fishermen, and to
form seamen. The poverty of the men at Dingle
and other places on the west and south-west coasts
make them able only to fit out canoes, to the almost
extinction of the sprit-boat and the hooker. The
consequence is, that the herring fishery is much on
the decline. And what can this wretched system
avail, with their few hundred fathoms of spilliard
line and the sceltane of hooks, on those abundant
fishing-grounds? It is not that they are unequal as
seamen and fishermen, but it is their poverty, *and
the absence of all encouragement to fisheries.* Compare
this with the vessels that fish the coast of Iceland, Norway, the Orkneys, and the Well-bank, the
Dogger-bank, and the Broad Forties—vessels ably
manned, well found, and with twelve miles of lines,
who fish the Dogger-bank in the North Sea, 150
miles from land, remaining months on the ground at
anchor or hove-to, weathering heavy seas and heavy
gales. A fine vessel I saw at Greenwich, of sixty-six
tons, had eleven miles of long lines, with hand-lines
and nets, had ample stowage between decks for salt

and curing fish, and could bring alive in her well 2,000 cod-fish.

" When Government aid and protection were given to our Newfoundland and Labrador fisheries, we had vessels of 250 to 400 tons working throughout four months of the year on the great banks, in dense fogs, and a perpetual and heavy swell. These employed a large number of seamen—they remained at anchor on the banks, veering out 120 fathoms of cable, and sometimes in heavy weather having 200 fathoms of cable on end. In gales they weighed and hove-to. Since the withdrawal of all encouragement, the trade is principally carried on, in the in-shore fisheries, by boats of from nine to fifteen tons. The encouragement given by the French Government of several millions of francs a year to the Newfoundland fishery, enable the French to keep on the banks vessels of 300 tons, manned by at least forty men in each, and found with seven to nine heavy anchors, and upwards of 800 fathoms of hemp cables. These vessels have each four to five large boats, that can stand heavy weather, lines that cover a great extent of ground, and numerous nets and fishing tackle ; 17,000 to 20,000 of these men return to France every winter, and are ready to serve the imperial marine. *The bounties given by France are not for the advancement of trade, but to create a navy !*

"In October, 1857, it was stated that Sir G. B.
Pechell, M.P. intended to bring under the consideration of Parliament, in the approaching session, the
whole question of the fisheries of France. Within a
few days of that month, twenty-one vessels had
arrived at Marseilles with 2, 357,000 kilogrammes of
cod-fish."

Companies have been tried at times, but being in
bad hands, and not having been worked properly,
they have proved failures, and this has greatly dis-
couraged any others from making the attempt. A
company was lately proposed, to fish the new fishing-
ground known as the Rockall Fishing Station. As a
description of this singular spot, I cannot do better
than append the letter written to *The Times* by Mr.
Dawson :—

From THE TIMES *of November* 2, 1861.

"SIR,—As I have received numerous letters from
so many of the principal towns in England, Scotland,
Ireland, and the Isle of Man, desiring information
about Rockall, what is the mode of fishing there,
what size of vessel is suitable, what lines are required, and what markets, stations, and harbours are
most convenient, &c., I will, with your kind permission,
give them, through the medium of *The Times*, all the

information of which I am in possession, and endeavour to point out the best method of developing its riches.

" The fishing-ground at Rockall, upon which Messrs. Rhodes, Gardner, and other masters of cod-fishing smacks, met with such extraordinary success in August last, and discovered such vast shoals of large, beautiful white cod, and numerous other fish, is a sandbank in the North Atlantic Ocean, of nearly 100 miles in length and forty in breadth. The rock which gives it a local habitation and a name, is situate in 57 deg. 35 min. N. latitude, 13 deg. 41min. W. longitude, and is of a rounded form, rising about eighteen or twenty feet above the sea. When viewed from a quarter of a mile distant, it has all the appearance in size of a round cornstack. The top is nearly flat, and was quite white with the offal of the numerous sea-birds that hatch upon it in summer. There is no other rock visible above water, but I understand that there is a reef of five or six miles in length, covered by from two to five fathoms of water. Mr. Bolton, of the *Howard*, thinks that the tides set in a circle round the rock, from the way the vessels drifted when fishing, but his stay was too short for ascertaining the truth of his conjecture.

" The nearest land to Rockall is the small island of

St. Kilda, one of the outermost of the Hebrides or
Western Isles of Scotland, and it is distant 136 miles.
There is no harbour, shelter, or business carried on
in St. Kilda, but it is advisable for ships going to
Rockall to take their bearings from it, otherwise the
rock is not easily found, being so small an object ; it
appears, when only a few miles from it, as a barrel
floating in that boundless sea.

"The method pursued by the smacksmen in fishing
at Rockall was the same as is usually practised by
them in the North Sea during summer.   The smacks
were stout welled ships, of from forty to fifty
tons register, with a crew of five men and four
apprentices.   They used hand-lines only, with a
leaden sinker and two hooks on each man's line.
Any offal did for bait ; the best was a piece of the
back fin of a tusk, cut to resemble a small fish.   This
bait being tough, it lasted for days on the hook.
After the fish were caught they were gutted, split,
and the heads cut off, and the backbone taken out as
far down as the vent, then salted and laid in layers
one above another until the space in the ship was
filled up.   They returned to Westray, and delivered
them to the merchants, who have long been the purchasers of their fish in that state, by the ton or
score.   *Some of the smacks were out twelve days from*

Westray to Rockall, but only five days on the fishing-ground, four days having been occupied in going and three days in returning. They had fourteen tons of cod each, for which they received 10l. per ton (140l. worth of fish caught in five days) ; but after those fish were dried and prepared for market, they were sold by the merchants, a few weeks after, for nearly double that amount. The heads and other offal (with the exception of the liver, which is the perquisite of the master) were thrown overboard at Rockall, a practice which cannot be too much condemned, as those fishermen very well know that they spoil their fishing-ground by doing so. Dry-bottomed ships suit better for this dead fishing than the welled smacks. The wells occupy so much space that there is little room left for holding fish, salt, &c., and the vessels consequently cannot remain long on the fishing-ground. The crews were also found to be few for Rockall, and their lines not strong enough for such large, heavy fish. Each man is provided with two hand-lines and a good supply of hooks; the lines require to be about 100 fathoms long. The very best line that I have ever seen (and practical judges say the same) for fishing purposes is that made by a recently-invented machine, said to be on an entirely new principle. The cord, from the regularity of the back

twist, never snarls nor goes out of twist; it is as
elastic as hair for snoods and imps; it must be in-
valuable, and a great *desideratum* to our fishing
community. It is prepared by a Mr. Hay, Renfrew
Lane, Glasgow.

" One of the best means of developing the riches
of Rockall would be by means of a company of
40,000*l*. or 50,000*l*., raised in 1*l*. or 2*l*. shares under
the Limited Liability Act, and to be called the Cod-
fishing, Oil, and Manure Company. Such a company could have three large ships, with twenty or
thirty men and boys in each ship, to remain there
fishing in all possible weather; and one ship as a
tender, to carry out fresh water and provisions and
salt to the stationary ships, and bring home to the
merchants or curing-station the fish caught by them;
and another one for the purpose of collecting and
carrying to the manure manufactory all the offal,
bodies of sharks, and other unsaleable fish; and one
welled smack could be employed in carrying live fish
for the fresh market: six ships in all—five dry-
bottomed and one welled smack. The stationary
fishing-ships should be supplied with a harpoon,
whale-boats, and line, also some small chain-tackle for
the sharks—their livers contain much oil. The ships
should also make medicinal cod-oil on board fresh

every day, as that commands the best price. It only
requires the cod-livers to be put into a dry tin pan,
and the pan placed inside a metal pot containing
water, which, being brought to the boil, heats the tin
pan as it were by steam, and causes the oil to exude
from the livers. When all is out it is taken and put
into flannel bags, and allowed to strain through them,
when it is pure for the market. These pans are very
simple and easy of management. I have seen them
made some years ago by Mr. T. Statham, tinsmith,
Eyemouth, Berwickshire, and used there by the Messrs.
Dickson, whose cod-liver oil, so prepared, was famed
for its sweetness and purity.

Some person, acquainted with gutting, splitting,
and salting fish will require to be on board every
ship going to Rockall. The company's welled
smack for carrying the live fish could be filled
up at Rockall in two days at most, with the
assistance of the stationary ships' crews, and thus
be kept carrying the fish alive to some suitable
railway harbour near the best market, where the
fish could be taken from the well, and forwarded
in boxes by rail in one or two hours. There is a
difficulty in getting such large fish to live, hauled
from such a depth, which can be overcome, where the
fish are so numerous, by adopting the plan used by the

Orkney men to catch lobsters. A net bag, the mouth of which is kept open round a large iron ring, a weight and some bait being secured in the centre of the bag, is let down to the bottom of the sea, when the fish, attracted by the bait, enter within the circumference of the ring, and if hauled quickly up the fish will be in the bag net, and can then be put into the wells without being blown or handled at all.

" One of the uninhabited Orkney Islands would decidedly be the best adapted for the manure manufactory and depôt, to which all the offal should be carried, as the effluvia would annoy no person. There are harbour dues here, and it is midway between the fishing-ground and the east coasts of Scotland and England; and, above all, any quantity of vegetable matter can be procured for mixing with the fish offal; and a large shed would have to be erected, and a kiln, for drying and driving out the superfluous water from the materials, built, and a mill put up for bruising and mixing them when dried and ready for market. Thousands of tons of far richer guano can be made by this means in one year, on the same principle and with the same materials as the climate of Peru has taken hundreds of years to produce. This would be a boon to agriculture, and give a large dividend to the shareholders. An American gentleman writes me that he has come to London for the establishing of such a manufactory in connexion with a company in the Gulf of St. Lawrence and New-foundland, to supply the farmers of this country with this manure, which experience has proved, he states, to be equal, if not superior, to the best Peruvian guano, and at a comparatively low price.

"There is no shelter, harbour, or landing-place at or near Rockall. The smacks that left Westray Bay returned to it again without requiring to call anywhere. This beautiful and well-sheltered bay of Westray, Orkney, has been long the rendezvous for cod-fishing smacks, and for the sale of their fish. It can be entered at any tide or wind, and there are no harbour charges. The Westray merchants are also prepared to buy all the fish brought. Some of the Westray fishermen accompanied the smack to Rockall, and all of them are well acquainted with splitting and drying for the markets. Stornoway, in the Island of Lewis, the property of Sir James Matheson, M.P., is a suitable place also for a station, but I am not aware of the accommodation to be got. There is a deep harbour at a place called Belderig, on the north coast of Mayo, in Ireland; it is about a mile square; large ships can enter and leave at any time of tide; it lies in 54 deg. 19 min. N. latitude, 9 deg. 34 min.

W. longitude. Its nearness and the prevailing winds make that place very suitable for curing-stations and depôts for ships fishing at Rockall; and when the railway is finished next year from Dublin to Castlebar, fish can be conveyed from Belderig to London in thirty-six hours. The proprietor, Mr. John Ross Foord, Rochester, Kent, England, states to me that he will be most happy to give every facility to parties wishing to erect stations, &c., and is willing to give masters and owners of vessels every information on the subject on applying to him.

"The previous letters in *The Times*, announcing the discovery of this extraordinary fishing-ground, have created a great sensation among the cod-smacksmen and all connected with these fisheries; and Captain John Rhodes, of the *Resolution*, has become the most popular man of his class from Grimsby to Gravesend, for we are informed that he never appears in public now in those places, but a crowd of men and boys gather at his heels, shouting 'Three cheers for Rockall!' and he is about to reach the very acme of English popularity, as his portrait is shortly to appear above the doors of a Rhodes Hotel and Rockall Coffee-room, in the good town of Grimsby, and no doubt the example will be followed by the other coast towns of Essex and Kent. The publicity of these letters has also been the means, already, of adding some 1,000*l*. sterling to the wealth of the community. A highly respectable and extensive firm in London, seeing the remarks about throwing the offal into the sea, wrote to me stating that they would purchase 10,000 cwt. of the roes of cod, and give as high as 11*s*. per cwt., if the fishermen would preserve them, to be used as bait on the west coast of France. They had previously been supplied from Norway, and had been paying annually to that country nearly 6,000*l*. for that which we were throwing away as an unsaleable commodity. Parties in Grimsby have now willingly come forward and agreed to supply them in future.

" I would again, in behalf of the fishermen, beg leave to call the attention of Government, through your influential paper, to this little-known Rockall, as buoys should be put upon the reef early in the spring, and a large vessel might be sent to cruise on that station for a season, to prevent casualties, or until the currents and tides become thoroughly known to the fishing-vessels. Surely it is as honourable and necessary to protect the large fleet that will assemble there in the spring, from the hidden rocks and the treacherous ocean as from any other enemy ! I am, Sir, yours very truly, F. DAWSON, M.D.

Broagh House, Westray, October 18, 1861."

I have lately heard that the anticipations of the inexhaustible abundance of fish to be found at Rockall, which were at first so confidently indulged in, have not been so fully realized by subsequent experience. Whether the deficiency is an actual and permanent one, or only temporary and accidental, time alone will show.

The most valuable fish which visits our coasts is, unquestionably, the Herring. In Norway, the strongest and most careful measures are adopted to keep this fish upon their coasts, and to induce it to multiply and return to them. Every facility that science and ingenuity can suggest is offered to its spawning in the numerous fiords, and the spawn and fry is not in any way disturbed or suffered to be molested, for fear of driving the fish elsewhere; and well may such measures be adopted, for in Norway there are 40,000 fishermen engaged in this fishery yearly. In Scotland, where the fishery is very extensive, there are said to be something like 70,000 persons engaged in fishing and curing, and 11,000 vessels of all sizes. Of course a very large proportion of these persons are curers, a vast number of them women, who have also other occupations.

To show further the magnitude of the interests involved in our fisheries, I may state that, according to the report of the Commissioners, in spite of the great depression existing in Ireland in 1860, there were no less than 53,714 men, 3,384 boys, and 14,182 vessels of all sizes, more or less engaged in fishing of various kinds The boats of course, as has been previously pointed out, are, for the most part, small craft, and far from as efficient as they might be, while the number of boys engaged appears to have fallen off from the year previous, which cannot but be looked on as a bad sign. I have no means of estimating the number of men and vessels engaged in England, but they must be considerable, as the fisheries on our north-west and south-east coasts are of great extent and importance. These figures will serve to show the reader the magnitude of the interests already involved, and it cannot be doubted but, by judicious management, they might be vastly increased.

Now, whether the management the fisheries meet with be judicious or no, I leave the reader to judge. In Scotland a Board exists for the protection of the herring fishery. Let us see what the fishmongers of Scotland, whose living is, to an extent, dependent on the breath of this Board, have to say to it. The following extract is taken from the speech of the chairman at the Glasgow fish-merchants' annual dinner :—

"But while I speak of herrings, I cannot allow this opportunity to pass without condemning a Board which has for its object the protection of the herrings. The Fishery Board was instituted at the beginning of this century, when all Europe was at war, and when the difficulty of manning the navy was much felt. A bounty of four shillings a barrel was paid the fishermen for every barrel of herrings cured; and in 1821 the Board disbursed 72,000*l.* for that object, which, with expenses (12,000*l.*), make 84,000*l.* as a bounty, or rather, I should say, as a bribe, for men to become sailors. Since 1830, the Government bounty has been withdrawn, and the operations of the Board have virtually ceased; but in courtesy to the Honorary Commissioners, it has been allowed to exist. So great has the demand been for fresh fish, and so inactive has become the Board of Fisheries, that the fishermen openly violate the laws by the use of illegal nets, at the risk of all consequences. You are all aware that last summer a bill for the better protection of the herring fisheries was brought into Parliament by the Lord Advocate and the Board of Fisheries, without anyone practically connected with the trade being consulted on the subject. The then existing law, which was never enforced, prohibited trawling, and the use of any other net than the regular inch mesh. The present bill was nothing more than a thirty years' bill of indemnity to the Fishery Board for the improper violation of all Acts, and handing them over the full control of the fisheries to do with as they pleased. In fact, the Lord Advocate and the Fishery Board did not object to the system of trawling, while the trade and public were strongly against it. Upon this point a committee in Glasgow was appointed to oppose the bill in Parliament; and thanks to the able advocacy of our Scotch members for making the present bill what it is, the title only of which is due to the Lord Advocate. The new bill, prohibiting trawling and enacting a close-time from the 1st of January to the 31st of May, has now been in operation several months, *and you all well know with what perfect indifference the Fishery Board has put the law in force. Trawling has gone on to a greater extent than ever.* Two of her Majesty's war-steamers are said to be continually in Loch Fyne and the Lochs, but we seldom hear of these vessels being far from Rothesay. The Fishery Board is either unable or unwilling to put the Act in force; for I cannot believe but that the two steamers now stationed on the west coast could have put down trawling in a week's time if they had had the commands to do so."

Such is the evidence publicly offered by practical

men, whose living depends upon the fishery. As regards the Board, I should by no means wish to see it done away with, as some of its functions are of a most useful and valuable nature. For example, before a cask of herrings is finally closed, an officer is appointed to examine it, to see that no unfit fish are packed away in it. Having ascertained this, he sees the cask headed, and affixes the Government brand to it; and so excellent has been the effect of this system, and so great is the reliance placed in that Government brand, that barrels of English herrings, thus marked, are taken without question or hesitation by merchants, even in the uttermost parts of Siberia, as readily as though they were hard cash. It is needless to say that the doing away with the brand, and abolition of this supervision, which has existed for so long a series of years beneficially, would not only open the way to frauds of all kinds, but the very change of system would shake the faith of these distant merchants, and would create suspicion, and would in a short time destroy both our position and our trade. I mention these points here, as it has been proposed to abolish the brand.

During the last session but one of Parliament, the Board obtained the power from the Government to suspend any of the clauses in the Act at its own pleasure. Now, in January 1861, the clause prohibiting trawling with small meshed nets was suspended, under the pretence of allowing the fishermen to catch sprats or garvies ; and the result was that, on the first morning on which this wholesome restriction was thus openly removed by the Board, four fishing-boats brought in, and sold as sprats, above 400,000 herring-fry. Now, had these fry been permitted to live a few months, they would have become herrings, and have been worth (setting the herrings at the rate of two a penny), between 800l. and 900l.—as sprats they would not, probably, fetch as many farthings ; but if this be the destruction of one night, what must be the havoc in a whole season ? Will it not be a marvel of marvels if there be any herrings left in a few years' time ?

This process it is which has destroyed the herring fisheries, and all the other fisheries upon so many of those magnificent Highland sea lochs, which, answering to the Norwegian fiords, but a few short years since rolled their tides of wealth and abundance to the very feet of the now almost starving Highlanders, who behold the lochs deserted by the herring, which has been driven away and exterminated by unfair fishing ; and not only by the herring, but by all the other fish which formerly attended upon it, and lived upon the spawn and fry to a great extent. It is not a difficult thing to drive the herring away from any locality, but who can bring them back again? The splendid lochs on the western Scotch coast, formerly teeming with fish, are now comparatively tenantless; and the herring the Highlander formerly got for the mere trouble of taking it, he now imports from Norway, and pays for in hard cash. I am not here objecting to trawling in *deep water*, where it can do no harm, but to trawling on the spawning-grounds.

It has been stated by able Ichthyologists that sprats are not the young of the herring, some difference existing in the position of the fins, and the belly of the one being serrated while the other is smooth; but a writer of an article in the *Cornhill Magazine*, some time since, stated that, from experiments he had made, he found that this latter peculiarity left the fish as it grew older, or towards herringhood, and he asserted that the sprat was neither more nor less than the herring-fry. I give the statement as it stands, neither vouching for nor denying it. Should it be true, the large numbers of sprats which are sent into our markets would very easily account for the great decrease which has taken place in herrings.

We have tolerably good evidence that other nations by no means share in our apathy as regards the interests of *their* fisheries. Witness the three nights' discussion in the French Parliament of matters affecting their fishings, and the expensive mission sent out by the French *Société d'Acclimatation* to Norway and elsewhere, as well as that of Monsieur Coumes to England, to collect facts concerning the fisheries. Witness the astuteness and attention of the Dutch towards them; the great care and strict laws with regard to salt-water fishings of the Norwegians themselves; and it certainly seems anomalous to find such little care taken by us of interests of a tenfold larger extent, though of a similar nature.

The great evil which our fisheries all around the coast suffer from is from these small-meshed trawlers being allowed to trawl close inshore, where the fry of all kinds of fish betake themselves for safety. Worked in such places, the small trawls destroy the spawn and fry of all the fish that inhabit our coasts to an extent which cannot be calculated, and, if it could, would be so incredible that few would be found who would believe it. But to give a slight notion of what can be done, I may state that from the small poke-net of a common shrimper on the Sussex coast I have seen, at almost every emptying of the net, as many as from

ten or a dozen to forty or fifty of the fry of soles.
turbot, plaice, or flounders, of from an inch and a half
to two inches in length. There would be, perhaps, a
score of these nets at work within sight at the same
time, and at the lowest computation they would be
emptied two score of times a day. Some of them
gather their shrimps while standing in the water, and
allow the rubbish and fry to fall back into it; but
many more empty their nets on the shore, and cast
the fry on the beach.

It is not easy to compute the mischief which
even these fishers in a small way do. But the
small-meshed trawl-nets are wholesale destroyers,
and should not be allowed to be worked under a set
depth of water; as they cannot save the fry, which
are smothered in the mass of weed which the net
collects, while the good fish they take are incon-
siderable, and the prawns, for which they are chiefly
worked, can be taken in the pots constructed for the
purpose, and which do no mischief.[1] The remedy

---

[1] I will instance further one case which has lately come under
my notice. On the coast of Suffolk, about the town of Aldeburgh,
there were formerly large quantities of codling, whiting, flounders,
and many other fish. These were so abundant, that it was only
necessary to cast a line into the sea from off the beach, when a good
take of these and other fish could be made; while a long line, with
a hundred or two of hooks, set at some distance from the shore,

here is plainly to prohibit trawling in shallow water, to place a penalty upon the destruction of fry, to appoint a fence-time, and to empower the coast-guard to enforce it. There is no other method, and the coastguard, as regards smuggling, have now really very little to do which is worth their employment; whereas in the protecting of our fisheries, and seeing that the proper regulations as regards the machinery, fence-times, &c. be enforced, they would render most valuable assistance, and they are to a small extent already occupied in this matter. The size of all fish which it is permissible to take is laid down in the Act of the 1st of Geo. I.; and under the sizes there laid down, it should not be permissible either to take fish, or to sell them, or have them in possession.

In looking further into the papers written by Mr. Andrews upon the Irish fisheries, I find a vast

would well repay the fisherman for his trouble. Visitors came to the spot as a convenient watering-place, and the fishermen in the summertime found that, by using their small trawls for shrimps, they could earn a trifling remuneration with very little trouble. These trawls were accordingly used, in two or three fathoms of water, on the banks where the fish naturally came to spawn; and the result of the persistence in this species of fishing has been, that the fish have in a great measure been driven from the spot, and line-fishing there is now not worth the trouble of prosecuting. There are many other places along the coast where the same result has ensued from a similar practice.

deal of valuable information in respect to trawling.
This information, I regret to say, is too extended and
diffuse to be given here; but I gather from it that,
owing to the want of proper boats and gear, and the
ignorance of the proper soundings and localities, vast
ranges of most valuable trawling-ground upon the
Irish coasts are utterly unproductive. And another
cause has contributed to render some of them comparatively so—viz., that boundaries were set by the
Fishery Board, where trawling was prohibited, upon
some of the very best and most productive spots,
owing to the ignorant and jealous prejudice evinced
by some of the small-boat fishermen, who could not
prosecute anything but the most meagre form of line
and net fishing.

In some places, as at Dingle for example, Mr.
Andrews had succeeded in establishing very remunerative fisheries, in which hundreds of men and
boys obtained an excellent livelihood. The mode of
fishing was greatly improved; craft of a superior
size and better gear introduced; and the number
of fishermen and boys were increasing rapidly, when
jealous clamour was raised by some ten or a dozen
half-fishermen — half-farmers, and the consequence
was, that they got the trawling prohibited on the
best grounds, leaving only the rocky and foul ground,

where it could not be prosecuted. I believe, however, that very lately some modification of this state of things was introduced by the Board; but a serious blow had been dealt to the prosperity of the fisheries and the fishermen, which they will take years to recover from. In Galway Bay, the same outcry was raised by the Claddagh men but lately, because better and larger boats than they possessed were trawling in the bay. In such cases, it is requisite that the Board should use the utmost discrimination in the rules and boundaries which they lay down, as well as in taking evidence upon all such matters.

It cannot be doubted, from the evidence afforded in the able papers so often referred to, that the Irish fisheries are capable of improvement to an extent now hardly dreamt of, and that a mine of wealth, sufficient to maintain the peasantry in affluence all round the coasts of Ireland, lies almost at their doors, now, comparatively speaking, unworked and unproductive.

There is another circumstance, besides the wasteful destruction of small fish, which is gradually but surely affecting our coast fisheries. Wherever mining operations are carried on, the rivers and brooks are first poisoned by them and all the fish killed; and the poisoned water in turn, emptying itself into the sea, carries down very strong deposits, which in time, being driven about and dispersed by the waves, has the effect of driving the fish off the coast. One instance of this, out of many, I will particularize. At Aberystwith, two rivers carry down from the lead mines strong poisonous deposits. Twenty or thirty years ago, before the mines were opened, the rivers abounded in fish, and the sea-coast adjacent was abundantly supplied with many kinds of sea-fish. Within the time specified, however, they have almost entirely disappeared for some miles above and below this place, though plentiful enough beyond the limit. At times, it is true that mackerel, dog-fish, &c. are caught there; but these are principally *mid-water fish*, and it is the ground-feeding fish that are mainly affected by these poisonous deposits.

There is one other fact in connexion with our sea fisheries that I must touch upon, and that is, the permitted infringement of our lawful boundaries, secured to us by treaty, on the part of French and Dutch fishing-boats. I have previously noted the action of the Government upon our fisheries in Newfoundland, but here we have a specimen of its inaction upon our own coasts. To such lengths has the supineness of our cruisers and the boundless impertinence of these fishermen carried them, that they have landed at our fishing villages by hundreds at a time and caused serious riots; while as regards the fishing upon our grounds, it has been practised to a very great extent indeed—fleets of French and Dutch boats taking the living out of the mouths of our poor fishermen, and often sailing through their nets and destroying their gear, regardless of the consequences, or the destruction they caused.

I was not satisfied with reports of these matters; but being in Northumberland during the herring season of 1861, I went to Bamburgh and North Sunderland, where these occurrences were taking place, and saw and inquired for myself, and consequently am able to give tolerably correct evidence of the facts. The French boats were in the habit of coming in and fishing within a mile of the shore, though the treaty limits are three miles. Now it seems, to say the least of it, a strange sort of reciprocity laid down in this treaty; for while French fishermen are permitted to fish within three miles of our shores, our fishermen are not permitted to fish within *three leagues of theirs.* The French boats had occasioned a good deal of damage and mischief to our boats, and it was not until a great outcry had been made by the press, that active measures were taken against the French boats, when a few of them were summoned and fined in small amounts.[1]

Now, it cannot for a moment be doubted but that the slightest hint from the Admiralty, or the department of the Government under which the cruisers are placed, as to the necessity of a little activity in putting down these irregularities, would result in their instant suppression. It avails nothing to say that the cruiser was away on other duty—here, or there, or anywhere—when these things occurred, and therefore did not see them. If one cruiser is not equal to the work, surely we are rich enough to support two or three, or half a dozen if it be necessary! These things should cease, or, rather, never have occurred: it is an affront put upon us, and a robbery upon our citizens—for a fisherman, like any one else, pays his taxes that he may be protected and enjoy the rights of a British subject; and for trumpery fishing-boats to venture upon such an impertinence on our own shores, again and again, may well cause us to doubt whether Britannia really does rule the waves.

Some years since my father, the late Captain John Morgan, R.N., had charge of the interests of

[1] One or two of the French boats were summoned and fined trifling amounts during the past season, but the fines are far too light to arrest the practice.

our oyster fisheries at Jersey for a period of nine years; and I have often heard him say, that if any of our boats happened to infringe the boundary, which would occur at times, the French cutters used to come down upon them and fire a shot at the boats, and on one or two occasions they killed some of our fishermen by so doing. What the practice is now will be shown by the following letter, extracted from *The Field:—*

"FRENCH ENCROACHMENTS ON ENGLISH FISHING-GROUNDS.

"SIR,—I was glad to see the observations on this subject in your impression of the 13th ult. The depredations committed on our fisheries on the north-east coast, by the powerful and strongly-manned luggers of the French fishermen, have become so systematic and extensive of late years, and have been so habitually winked at by the naval authorities, whose duty it is to repress them, that our own fishermen have suffered severely in consequence.

"It is not, however, by the infliction of paltry penalties of 5*l.* each, that they are to be deterred from such malpractices: one night's successful fishing on our banks would more than amply reimburse them in that amount, to say nothing of the chance—

which is fifty to one in their favour—of escaping unmolested. I was at Dieppe during the spring of last year, when the avisos *Corse* and *Pelican*, charged with the protection of the fisheries on that station, were daily bringing in English fishing-craft which they had captured; and there were at one time lying in the harbour no less than seventeen Colchester trawling-smacks, which had been seized for trespassing on the French oyster-beds. They lay in a line along the whole of one side of the inner harbour, and their clean lines and taut smart rig presented a striking contrast to the ugly, lumbering luggers and sloops of the Poletais fishermen.

" These poor fellows were kept there in custody for ten days or a fortnight, and then only dismissed after taking from them their trawl-ropes, trawls, and all superfluous lines and rigging, to the value of 30*l*. or 40*l*., from each boat—leaving them, in fact, just what was necessary for them to find their way home with, and no more. I don't mean to defend them: they admitted that they were acting illegally, and with a full knowledge of the penalty they incurred; but one of them said to me, 'It's hard enough work for us to earn our grub, sir, with only three men and a boy on board, while a French craft the same size carries eight men and four boys, with half their wages paid by their Government, and a bounty on all the fish they bring in besides, and fishes in our grounds when and where they likes;' and hard enough I thought it. At all events, what is sauce for English is sauce for French fishermen.

"I presume the usage of confiscating tackle and implements is warranted by the international fishery-treaties, or the French authorities would not practise or our Consul at Dieppe permit it. Our fisheries are very inadequately protected, and these regulations are not enforced by the officers in charge of them with the same strictness as on the other side of the Channel. Surely, our gunboats would be better employed in this duty than lying in the Medway until their bottoms are so encrusted with oysters that they have to be dubbed off with shipwrights' adzes! (*Vide* the *Times* of the 24th.) If, however, on the rare occasions when French craft are caught in the fact, our north-country magistrates would mete out the same justice to them, by impounding all their nets and spare tackle, it would necessitate their going home to refit, and prevent their trespassing on our grounds, for that season's fishing at all events.

"J. WICKEY."

I need not comment upon the above letter further
than to say, that I believe that such treatment of our
fishermen is entirely illegal and unjustified by any
treaty whatever, and is an arbitrary exercise of power
which, were such a thing attempted towards a French
boat, would produce correspondence and diplomatic
uproar.   To show how productive of mischief the
laxity and supineness of our cruisers is, I may mention that, a short time since, an affray ensued between
one of our Ramsgate fishing-boats and a French boat,
in which one of the Frenchmen lost his life; and the
case is, I believe, still pending for inquiry.

In considering our sea fisheries, the formation and
protection of oyster-beds is a subject which ought
to receive the special attention which so delicious
and valuable an edible deserves.   In England, in
certain favoured localities, as the eastern coast,
companies have had the cultivation of oysters in
hand, and are making a handsome revenue from
supplying the markets; but they are few, compared with the wide fields which are open to such
cultivation.   In Ireland, the attention of many
gentlemen has been particularly turned to this
product; and during the year 1860, seventeen
gentlemen have obtained licences for the planting of
artificial oyster-beds on various parts of the coasts.

A suitable locality having been chosen and obtained, the cost of planting and preserving an oyster-bed is small when contrasted with the enormous profits reaped from it. One of the worst foes that oyster-bed proprietors have to dread is frost, which destroys vast numbers in the shallower waters. Still, the profits are very large, and the subject is well worth the more general attention of proprietors by estuaries, sea lochs, and such localities as are favourable for the planting of oyster-beds. The French are largely engaged in this branch of pisciculture.

The very best oysters we get are the Natives, as the oysters of Whitstable and Colchester chiefly are denominated. The small oysters or spawn, called in the trade "spat," is collected all round the coast, and deposited in the oyster-beds, in localities most favourable to its development, where the greatest care is taken of the beds until the fish are fit for sale, when the oysters are dredged up, and any spat which may be adhering to them is removed and returned to the water. Vast quantities of oysters are brought from Jersey, where the oyster-beds are unusually large and fertile. The coarsest and worst oysters we obtain are the Channel oysters.

The close-season, at any rate as regards the better kinds of oysters, is well kept. Probably one good

reason for this is, that the subject of the cultivation
of oysters has been studied and is well understood
by the few people who carry out their cultivation,
and also that soon after it commences oysters are
not in the best condition for eating; and the old
saying about their being not eatable save when there
is an R in the month, is so impressed on the minds of
the public, that the probability is that the sale would
hardly be remunerative. Moreover, the coastguard
are always somewhat active upon this point.   In
some places, however, the coarser oysters, such as one
sees about the bridges of London retailed at a penny
a lot, are dredged for all the year round: of course
the practice is a ruinous one.

There is a species of oyster in America, which is
said to be unusually delicious.   There could not be
any great difficulty in acclimatizing this shellfish in
England, if it were thought desirable and found to be
suitable.   There is also another shellfish held in great
estimation in America, which we might possibly cultivate to advantage—viz., the Clam, of which there
are several varieties: at any rate, we might try them.
Indeed, there are many members of the Crustacea,
besides those which we already have, which doubtless
might be used by us with advantage; and considering
the hundreds of small rivers and harbours we have

all around our coasts, where such cultivation might easily and advantageously be carried out to any extent, it is perfectly wonderful that such facilities are not made available for the production of food. With butcher's meat at 10*d.* a pound, anything which will serve to relieve the pressure should be taken advantage of.

Of anything like the cultivation of lobsters, crabs, and such members of the Crustaceæ we have so little knowledge, that it may be said to be still an occult or unknown science, though there cannot be a doubt but that artificial means of rearing and feeding them might easily be employed with success. To my knowledge it has never even been tried.

On many parts of the Continent, and particularly in Italy, large salt-water lakes have been made, or are utilized, for the purposes of pisciculture. These works are, for the most part, the remains and the result of ancient industry. The singular lagune at Commachio, on the Adriatic, is a peculiar instance of what art can do to assist nature in this respect. Originally, the spot was a marsh, intersected by small rivulets; at the outlet of these rivulets small islands, half submerged, lay close upon the coast. These rivulets were collected into a canal; the shallow pools made into

one large lagune; the islands connected and raised
by means of wickerwork, &c., which made a laby-
rinth, at every outlet of which certain traps were set.
The waters of the canal were turned into this lagune.
The fish from the sea enter through the traps into the
brackish water to spawn, but cannot return; and vast
quantities of eels, mullets, and other fish are thus
captured, a large stock always being kept up in the
lagune.

The Lucrine Lake is another specimen of what can
be done with oysters, but the salt lake of Fusaro,
which I have previously referred to, is a more singular
instance still.   This lake, which is situated between
the Lucrine Lake, the ruins of Cumæ, and the point
of Missene, was originally an extinct volcano, and at
times, even now, the sulphureous exhalations penetrate
the waters.   About forty years ago, the entire stock
of oysters in the lake was killed from this cause, and
the lake had to be restocked.   It is about a league
in circumference, and from three to six feet deep in
the middle.   The bottom is muddy, and is dotted
over with large stones or fragments of rocks, to which
the oysters may attach themselves; and round about
these stones large stakes, which project above the
water, are stuck into the soil—not so tightly, however,
but what they can be withdrawn.   From these stakes

to others extend lines or cords, and from these cords at intervals are suspended faggots, to and within which the spawn of the oyster, when first hatched, can attach and ensconce itself until safe from any outward danger. The use of these faggots and stakes is important, as when the young of the oyster is first hatched, it scatters in all directions, until it finds something to which it can safely attach itself. Meantime it is the prey of every fish or marine creature that can take it, while vast numbers perish from other circumstances; and were it not for the fact that each female oyster is said to give forth yearly from one to two millions of young, the stock, under the calls that are made upon it by man, must rapidly diminish. When about three years old the oyster becomes edible.

When they wish to obtain oysters at Lake Fusaro, they either break them off the stones with hooks, or pull up the stakes or faggots, and detach such as they require with their hands. This method of fishing, instituted by the ancients, is in practice to the present day; and the hint has not been lost upon the French, who have imported the plan to Marennes, while a system very similar to that at Commachio has been instituted at the Basin d'Arachon.[1] We have few, if

[1] The following account of what is being done by the French at the Ile de Ré was lately published in the columns of *Galignani:*—

" M. Coste

any, of such salt-water nurseries and ponds in England, although such ponds abound around our coasts, and there is scarcely a harbour or a river's mouth where

"M. Coste has just communicated a paper to the Academy of Sciences on the progress of his artificial oyster-beds on the western coast of France. Several thousands of the inhabitants of the island of Ré have been for the last four years engaged in cleansing their muddy coast of the sediments which prevented oysters from congregating there ; and as the work advances, the seed wafted over from Nieulle and other oyster localities settles in the new beds, and, added to that transplanted, peoples the coast, so that 72,000,000 of oysters, from one to four years old, and nearly all marketable, is the lowest average per annum registered by the local administration —representing, at the rate of from twenty-five to thirty francs per thousand, which is the current price in the locality, a sum of about two millions of francs, the produce of an extremely limited surface. That the waves or currents carry the seed of oysters is a well-known fact, since the walls of sluices newly erected are often covered with them. In the island of Ré the existence of the oyster-beds, however, no longer depends upon this contingency, they being now in a state of permanent self-reproduction. The distinction of oyster-beds into those of collection and those of reproduction is quite unnecessary, since the property of reproduction belongs to them all. In some localities it is sufficient to prepare the emerging banks for collection to see them soon covered with seed ; but in other places nothing would be obtained without transplanting proper subjects, an operation which by no means impairs their reproductive qualities. The concession of emerging banks is anxiously applied for by the inhabitants of the coast, the more so as improvements in the working of this branch of trade are of daily occurrence. Thus Dr. Kemmerer, of Ré, covers a number of tiles with a coating of a kind of mastick, brittle enough to enable him to detach the small oysters from it. When this coating is well covered with seed, he gets it off all in one piece, which he carries to the something of the kind might not with the utmost ease be carried out. I know of one small pool, near Titchfield, at the mouth of Southampton Water, where lobsters are placed; and this is a mere stew, in which they are kept for a few days until required. There are, however, as I have said, numberless places where fortunes could be realized, and vast stores of food provided for the people.

There are many other species of fish and kinds of fisheries on our coasts, which I might perhaps touch upon with advantage; but it is not my purpose at present, while the subject possesses so little general interest, to go at all deeply into it. I merely point to the state and treatment of the sea fisheries, and the general means whereby they may be improved. At some future period possibly, when the subject has challenged the notice and inquiry of the public, and become more popular, it may be worth while to go somewhat more particularly into it.

place where the seed is to grow. The same tile he coats a second time, and so on, as long as the seed will deposit upon it. In short, wherever the violence of the currents and the instability of the bottom do not present irresistible obstacles, the cultivation of oysters has become a lucrative business."

CHAPTER XI.

ON THE COOKING OF FISH.

I WILL now touch briefly on a branch of my subject which appears to me one of no little importance: I allude to the cooking of fish generally. Upon our methods of cooking the better sort of fish, save as regards the waste committed when cooking them, I need not touch. A Blackwall dinner is, of itself, evidence sufficient that our great cooks know the art to some extent; but it is in our little cooks that we fall so terribly off from that which should be.

Take the subject in its broad sense, what can be worse than the cookery of the great mass of the poor? Literally, they know nothing about cooking; and the producing of simple, palatable, wholesome, and inexpensive dishes is a profound mystery to them. Many points of distinction have been set forward between savage-life and what is termed civilization. Perhaps none is so characteristic and striking as the preparing of food, or "cookery," in the two states; and taking it as a test, the great bulk of our lower classes have little to brag of. The veriest savage that roams the North or South American wildernesses, the most uncivilized and unknown among the amphibious islanders of the Pacific, know better what they put into their stomachs and how to prepare it than our poorer countrymen do. It is a question if there is any human being on the face of the globe, barely excepting the Bosjesman of Australia or the Earthman of the Andes, who is so badly off in cookery knowledge as the English labourer. It may be that excess of civilization has completed our cycle in this respect, and brought us again to the bottom round of the ladder. I think that there is no greater evidence of the decline of character in England than the state of cookery knowledge amongst the lower classes. A knowledge of economical cookery, and the practice of it constantly by the wives, sisters, and mothers of labouring men, argues domestic duties properly fulfilled—industry, intelligence, and home ties and relationships drawn closer and purified by the fulfilment of those duties. It makes up, in fact, the sum of all that is worth living for in life. It may be much for the rich, but how incalculably more for the poor!

What ensues from that dirty-drab practice, begot
by unions and pauperism, of putting a pinch of tea
in the pot and serving that debilitating wash out to
the labourer, instead of a good, wholesome, cheap,
and strengthening *bouilli* for his dinner?[1]   Why, as
it saves trouble and aids gossip, it saves the woman
the only opportunity of a healthful use of the small
amount of brains she does possess, in the study of
how she can best provide something answering the
above description for her husband's, son's, or brother's
dinner: it results in the ignoring of the art of cookery,
and the necessity of practising or performing any
duties at all: it results in fearful waste of our resources.   It drives the husband to the beer-shop, and
often the wife too, to supply, by an artificial, unsus-
taining, and poisonous stimulus, the absence of what
should be supplied by food judiciously prepared.   It
must proceed eventually to the destruction of social
womanly respect and functions, of manly gratitude
for pains bestowed—to the breaking up of all home
feelings, ties, and virtues.   It must debase mankind

[1] Even supposing that, by way of strengthening himself, he takes
beer—what is *that* beer?   Granting, at the very best, that it be
made from malt and hops, it is a very bad substitute; but granting
it to be what publichouse beer in the country usually is, it is
practically gout, gravel, stone, dropsy, or any other disease which
poisons are most likely to generate.

to something below the beasts—to a creation without a purpose—human, but without human aims. It is not easy to conceive what a being can be which has lost the great type of its race—which belongs neither to savage life nor civilization—which cultivates the virtues of neither but the vices of both Intelligence, understanding, and self-respect must all be gone before these things will go ; and what can be the end if it be not a seething mass of feculent humanity, whose millennium will be universal drunkenness, and whose church a pot-house? What a fine satire it is upon civilization to hear a talk of plans for "Moral Cottages," and to find our Legislature actually busy with a "Labourers' Cottages Bill :" as if legislation could be expected to supply the loss of habits of housewifery, cleanliness, order, sobriety, and morality —as if character can be manufactured by Act of Parliament as easily as it can be unmanufactured !

But while we deplore the loss of this knowledge among the *labouring* class, we must not think that it does not affect the middle and even the upper classes. It must be remembered that it is from these lower classes that we draw our servants ; and it is now so much the fashion to make such very fine ladies of the daughters of the middle and upper classes, that the slightest knowledge of domestic

matters—particularly of anything so very low as
cooking—is scouted indignantly. How can a lady
who murders Mendelssohn or Beethoven five or six
hours per diem, who destroys crayons by the fasces,
or the nose upon Aunt Sally, or even longsuffering
Time in The Park, for sundry other hours, &c. &c., be
expected to bestow a thought upon anything so
utterly useless, degrading, and out of her sphere?
And thus this most vital matter, which has so much
to do with the health and peace of families in detail,
and the wellbeing even of nations in the aggregate,
is left to the ignorant stupidity of the modern
English servant, whose habits in respect to cookery
are, for the most part, of so wasteful a nature as to
be almost criminal. It is not too much to say, that
of all the food cooked in England one-fourth is
wasted, utterly wasted—thrown to the dust-hole and
the dogs. I could devote whole pages to the useful
consideration of this subject, but I am compelled to
confine my attention here to fish only.

There are many fish, which inhabit both salt and
fresh water, which we now reject as worthless; as if
anything which an Allwise Providence has sent for
our use could be worthless. The reason that we reject
these fish is because we do not know how to cook
them, or what particular use to put them to. The very

worst fish that swims, the most bony and apparently inedible of fish, contains nourishing properties to a large extent: for example, they may be made into most excellent and palatable soup, if flavoured according to taste, with very, very little trouble or expense indeed. Having boiled a huge mass of cod's head, or a turbot, we, as soon as possible, throw the liquor down the sink; whereas if that liquor were used again, when cool the second time, it would be a strong jelly. The skins and membranes of fish, for the most part, contain the strongest of gelatine. Isinglass, which produces even a stronger jelly and more nourishment than gelatine, is but a preparation of the sound of the sturgeon and other fish; and isinglass is given, much as cod-liver oil is, not only as a nourishing, but further as a strengthening food.

We do not throw away any portion of beef and mutton because it is coarse, tough, and flavourless; it is too expensive for that. We call it gravy or stock-meat, and we extract its juices by boiling; and why should we condemn any fish, when the coarsest and most flavourless of them can be turned to the best account also, by being used in a similar manner? A little pepper, a little salt, a dash of vinegar, and a sprig of herbs, is all that is required to turn barbel and chub into very good and enjoyable soup—not that

barbel or chub are by any means inedible of themselves, as I have often experienced; for, well cleaned,
with the backbone cut out, with pepper, salt, butter,
a slice of lemon, or a few drops of vinegar, they are
palatable if they are properly grilled.   These fish,
and many others, are constantly and chiefly used by
the Jews, who are infinitely better cooks than we
are, but from whom we nevertheless make no attempt
to learn the art of cooking the fresh-water fish which
are so excellent on their tables.

With regard to fish-soups, these are not generally
in favour in this country, for the reason that they
are not generally known.   If they were, there can
be no question that people would prefer materials
which cost but a tithe of the price of those they
at present employ, and contain, at least, as much if
not more nourishment, and which are also to the full
as pleasant to the palate; while it must always be
borne in mind that the increased use of the one
would tend to cheapen the other, and bring it more
readily within reach.

There is another way of preparing fish common in
Norway, whereby the worst and most bony of fish
may be made excellent food of.   The flesh of the fish
is partially boiled and then taken from the bones,
and the whole compressed, with some few common

herbs and spices, into a cake, which is baked, and is by no means to be despised.

We have a vast variety of most admirable fish included in our Fauna, and it is doubtful if any country in the world can equal us in this respect. We have waters unlimited in extent, both salt and fresh: rivers by thousands and thousands of miles, and lakes, ponds, canals, and other waters to the extent of hundreds of thousands of acres; and a great question is now beginning to dawn upon the minds of the workaday world of scientific naturalists and others—viz., what do we do with them? what do they yield? and what ought they to yield?

Is the land more naturally prolific than the water? Assuredly not. Two, or twenty, or two hundred acres of water will produce double the weight of animal food that two, twenty, or two hundred acres of land will, if as carefully tilled, and with this striking difference— that in the case of the production as regards land, there are very heavy working and other expenses; in the case of water there are comparatively few. Fish, even if left to themselves, will eat and grow, and nature will provide the means of sustenance, without either barns or stables, teams or fences, seeds or farming implements, or even draining: nay, in this instance, draining (if one felt inclined to make a grim joke) might be held decidedly injurious, as indeed is another rather large item in farming—viz., manures ; nor will fish property be subject to panics and convulsions. No one will speculate for a rise in carp, turbot, or trout ; no treaties of reciprocity can well give away our inland fisheries ; and those of commerce will not put all sorts of internal or external *ad valorem,* or prohibitory, or any other duties upon them—at least I hope not. They are our own produce, and worth so much per pound in the market on any day we like to sell them ; and if we do not sell them, why, we shall not lose by keeping them, for they cost us no money to feed, as do bullocks or sheep. If we have enough to export, they are a source of exchange and wealth, and will relieve our overtaxed industry ; or, at least, the effect of a large introduction of fish into our home provision-markets would speedily influence the price of every other production.

I have, in the foregoing pages, briefly reviewed the subject of our fisheries, and pointed out the various means which may be employed, and the best kind of investigations to make, and of experiments to conduct, in order that they may become a great mine of wealth to us; and I trust that the explanations and advice I have here offered may be found useful to those who are studying this question with the same views and wishes as myself.

APPENDIX.

APPENDIX.

I.

REASONS FOR THE DECREASE OF SALMON.

THE decrease of salmon is not a matter of yesterday, but may be traced back during a period of more than a quarter of a century, though undoubtedly that decrease has of late years progressed with alarming rapidity. If we take our average of the fishings over a reasonable period, we shall find that the mode of fishing adopted in Scotland and Ireland, but now, happily, for the most part abolished in England, is ruining those fisheries. When I speak of a reasonable period, I do not mean to confine it to any five, ten, or fifteen years, but to take it, as we only fairly can do, by the changes that have taken place in the methods of fishing.

For example, some twenty years ago, the Irish fisheries, by poaching, &c., were in a very reduced state. Laws were passed, and the rivers put under the management of officers appointed to see to them. In a very few years the fisheries improved wonderfully; but as they began to improve, and the style of fishing began to pay well, fixed nets, hitherto but little known on the Irish coasts, began to make their appearance. The more the fisheries improved the more these nets increased, and to such a degree that the rivers are beginning to suffer very severely. Small rivers are entirely extinguished by them, larger ones do not pay the up-stream proprietors for looking after them; *and poaching can never be suppressed, if the up-stream proprietors do not strenuously set their faces against it.* The fisheries in Ireland in the last three years show a considerable diminution rather than an increase, and this diminution cannot but go on increasing.

The system is manifestly ruinous, unfair, and illegal.[1] Suppose I own a river fifty miles long, I incur a great expense and a vast amount of trouble to get up a stock of salmon. The salmon go down to the sea, and some fellow who has hired fifty yards of seabeach runs out a fixed net half-a-mile long, and catches nearly every one of my fish. I have spent money and trouble for nothing; the stranger has ruined my river and destroyed all the salmon; and finding that it does not pay to fish his net longer, he takes it up and goes elsewhere to repeat his destruction. This is, actually and literally, what has been and is occurring in Ireland.

---

[1] Fixed nets and stake-weirs have been declared illegal by three judges, two concurring with Baron Pennefather in that judgment. Most of the estuary fisheries of Ireland are held by the public by a common-law right, and no one has therefore any right to obstruct or do away with any part of that right; nor can any act of parliament confer such a right. This judgment has been confirmed on several occasions.

According to the old laws of Ireland, all such nets were declared illegal, and actions were sustained against them. It was not until some few years ago that an act was passed to legalise them, though, as is shown in the note at p. 240, the act cannot legalise them where they interfere with a common-law right. In Scotland they are illegal now, save by prescription or immemorial use. If a sufficient quantity of fish are not allowed to run up a river to stock it, the river must decrease rapidly in production ; for vast as is the natural fecundity of the salmon, yet so numerous are its enemies, and so large a part of the watery creation prey upon its spawn and fry, that barely one solitary ova in every thousand deposited produces a full-grown salmon. Were this not the case, of course a dozen pairs of fish would stock a river; as it is, hundreds are required.

Salmon run up at all periods of the year : even in December, clean fish are often found running into unobstructed rivers. Every salmon in the sea would enter some river or other if not prevented, and when once in the river, he becomes an easy, nay a certain, prey to the nets or cruives. Now the earlier fish, usually called spring-fish, or those which run into the rivers in January, February, and March, are by far the most valuable to the rivers, and for the following reasons: Being early spawners, their progeny in turn become early fish, and in the early months of the year salmon is scarce, and fetches a very high price They are, too, usually large fish : added to this, the weather being cold, salmon will travel further, and will keep longer, and remain altogether in better condition. These facts show that particular attention should be shown to these fish, and that their breed should be encouraged as much as possible. This can only be done by allowing the earliest fish to run up free, by opening the fishing at the mouths of rivers a month later than usual. But the very facts above detailed afford also the cause of these fish being much more keenly sought after; and the result of this keenness is that in many rivers where they formerly abounded they are become extinct, while in others they struggle up few and far between, and hold but a doubtful existence at the best.

If it were possible to say how many fish are sufficient to stock a river well, and to let so many run up to fulfil that office; nay, if it were possible to deal with and count our shoals of salmon, as a farmer does his flocks of sheep and his oxen, we might reduce this point to a matter of calculation and figures, and become extremely practical and arithmetical over it. But it is *not* possible, and therefore the best and only way is to give the fish a reasonable and fair—*indeed, a favourable chance rather than the reverse* —of getting up to the head-streams without let or hindrance in good time. But do we do so? Nay, we rather wage a war of utter extermination against the salmon. Any one who has seen the ingenious variety and the multitude of engines set up on our coasts, estuaries, and rivers to bar the progress of and capture our salmon, will be filled with wonder that a single salmon ever escapes them.

To commence with the rivers. In every favourable pool and stream we have draught-nets of immense capacity,

worked one over the other incessantly at all hours, to inter-
cept and sweep on shore the fish that are running up ; we
have nets which are half fixed—that is, fixed at one end,
and extended across the stream : against these the salmon
strike, and the end of the net is immediately brought
round, so that the salmon are enclosed and dragged on
shore ; we have nets of a somewhat similar nature, which
are lifted up from below ; we have nets of every variety and
construction, worked at weirs (by which the fish are stopped
and gathered together in shoals) and elsewhere, much too
numerous to mention, for the ingenuity of man has been
racked to discover and adapt them to the work in the most
murderous fashions.   We have also fixed erections, some of
brush faggots, wattled stakes, and other materials, extending across the stream as far as may be practicable, against
which the salmon in its upward progress strikes ; and when
seeking to pass beyond the obstruction on the outside, they
become entangled in a bag, or in a maze of chambers, ending
in a species of trap similar to an eel or a funnel-mouthed
mouse-trap, from which there is practically no escape. We
have stages and ranges of baskets, like large wicker eel-pots,
into which the fish readily passes, and from which, when
they are perfectly adapted, nothing even of shrimp size can
escape alive.[1] We have cruives ; and here I must explain,
for the benefit of the general reader, what cruives are.

[1] Models of all these machines are in the possession of the Association for the Preservation of the Fisheries of Great Britain and
Ireland, 14, Regent Street—an excellent association, deserving of
every encouragement and support. These models were exhibited at
the International Exhibition, where they formed a very attractive
and instructive spectacle.

A weir is first erected, either entirely across the river or such portion as may be fishable, and over this the salmon cannot pass.   In this weir are left certain gaps, through which the stream flows : in these gaps are fixed the cruives or traps.   The cruives are composed of wooden bars in frames : these are called hecks or haicks.   The up-stream face of this cage is simply a vertical row of bars, so close together that they are impassable, save to the smallest grilse.   Formerly the Scotch law insisted that they should be set three inches apart, so that any fish under 8lbs. or 10lbs. in weight could pass through.   The old law of England also made fish of 6lbs. or 7lbs. in many of the rivers undersized fish, which it was illegal to take. The down-stream face of the cruive, through which the salmon must pass first in its upward progress, is made of two frames of bars, which are set so as to slant inwards until they meet ; one of these frames works loosely upon an upright spindle, so that when the salmon presses against it, it opens and lets him through, but closes behind him by the mere pressure of the stream.   The ground-plan of this trap will represent a square or rather oblong figure, with a triangle cut out of the lower face or base of it.

Once in these traps, there is no escape for poor salmon : the landing-net and a knock on the head, with a place on the icehouse floor, are his portion.   The traps are visited every morning and evening by men with large landing-nets, with which they are swept, and every fish is lifted out. I have seen from a dozen to thirty fish constantly taken in one of these cages at ordinary seasons, and when there is a great run of salmon on, of course the take is proportionably larger.

The old laws of Scotland required that a certain portion of the weir in the centre of the river should always be left open to the free passage of the fish. This was called "the king's gap or share." They also enforced what is called "the Saturday slop," when for a certain period, embracing the Sunday, the whole of the traps were thrown open, so that a perfectly free passage should be left. These arrangements, being properly and fairly enforced, always permitted a sufficient number of fish to run up to stock the river. It might, however, be necessary in the present day, as our fisheries are so much reduced, and the nets have much increased, and the drainage has so much altered the duration of floods, to enlarge the gap somewhat, and to lengthen the duration of the "Saturday slop" (at any rate for a time[1]), in order that a larger number of fish might be permitted to run up, that the rivers might be the quicker and better restocked, as has been done in the English Salmon Law.

Lastly, we have those most destructive engines of all, called stake and bag nets. The first of these is a net of a certain depth, extending vertically upon stakes, and ending like the brush-weir, in a maze of chambers. These stakes are carried out as far as the shore and depth of water will permit ; and if the stake-nets be not destructive enough, beyond this, a net is often carried out a great distance further by means of floating leaders and anchors, and is called

---

[1] By the new Scotch law, the "Saturday slop" is extended to thirty-six hours. The English, however, is forty-two hours.

a bag-net. These nets are set at right angles, or at a more suitable angle to the shore, and all fish seeking the rivers along the coast must strike against them. A great many fish are thus taken, and others are driven out to sea; and as these implements are usually employed near the mouths of rivers, the few fish which are not taken are driven from the river which they are seeking, and are, in all probability, put past the mouth of the river altogether; and when they again draw in to the shore for the purpose of entering the river, probably heavy in spawn, they come against some other net on the other side of their river, and if they have again the good luck to escape the maze of chambers, they are driven out to sea again; and thus they are kept in the sea for weeks and weeks over their natural time, a prey to the seals, sharks, and other predaceous animals, which always swarm near stake-nets, and during the residence of the salmon in the salt-water, take heavy and incessant toll of them. Such is the voracity and determination of the seal in pursuit of salmon, that they will rob the nets in the very face of the fishermen; and the destruction thus caused, and the number of salmon yearly lost to the consumer, from the fish being kept in the salt-water for an undue length of time, is something enormous in the total; and if they spawn it is in the tidal part of the river, probably in brackish or deep water, or in some other spot quite unsuited to the development of the ova, and thus the spawning is lost.

Some of these nets have seven or eight heads or sets of chambers, and extend out from the shore for nearly a mile. One of the most destructive species of mischief caused by them, where they are set near the mouths of rivers, is the enormous numbers of salmon-fry or smolts which they kill. Jammed together in masses of wrack and sea-weed, thousands on thousands are sacrificed in a tide ; and I have heard it stated on good authority, that on an occasion when one of the fishermen in the Beulay Firth waded out to attend to the net, that by the net in many places *he waded knee-deep in dead smolts, while the ground for a considerable distance about the net was literally silvered with their scales !* After this, can any one wonder at salmon decreasing ? The wear-and-tear of gear in this mode of fishing is very great ; indeed, it is the most expensive as well as the most destructive of all the modes of fishing. These nets, too, cannot well be made to observe close-time, even if one be appointed, as in very rough weather it may be impossible to remove any portion of them for weeks and weeks together ; and if stress of weather be permitted as an excuse for not opening them, every breeze will be so construed. It is not too much to say, that fixed nets have been the chief cause of the damage done to our salmon fisheries, and *it is impossible thoroughly to regenerate those fisheries while they are permitted to exist.*

By the law of England and the old laws of Ireland and Scotland, they are or were, as I have said, illegal. They are a comparatively modern invention, and the failure of our salmon fisheries may clearly and distinctly be traced, step by step, from the time of their first introduction ;[1] and they

[1] A singular proof of this is in the last report of the Irish Fishery Board. During the last three years, in consequence of the

ought, as a matter of justice to the other proprietors of fisheries, whose prospects they are destroying and have destroyed—as a matter touching the common profit of the realm—as a matter of destruction to the best and most valuable fish which we have, and a most important branch of the nation's food and resources, *to be done away with utterly.*

If they are done away with, in a very few years good salmon will be 6*d.* a pound, instead of from 1*s.* to 3*s.* 6*d.* We now import salmon from Holland very largely, and the fish are indifferent and flavourless compared to our own; and I am informed by one of the largest Billingsgate salesmen, that were it not for this importation, and were we to rely upon our own salmon for a supply, salmon would now, in this month of May, 1861, in which I am writing,[1] be not less than *five shillings per pound !* This statement ought to tell its own story: it ought to startle us into activity. Five shillings per pound ! for an article of food which does not cost one farthing to produce !! In fact, the salmon consumer may consider that he pays a tax of from 6*d.* to 3*s.* a pound to the fixed engines for salmon-slaying, while the great bulk of the nation are deprived of salmon altogether by them.

The close-time, during which salmon shall be allowed

increase in the value of salmon, there has been a regular and steady increase of bag and stake nets, amounting altogether to some 200. Just as these nets have increased, so in exact proportion the take of salmon has steadily and regularly decreased. This fact speaks volumes.

[1] This portion of my work was written at the above date, and as it serves to support the argument, I leave the date still standing.

to deposit their spawn unmolested, is also a matter of great importance. In the great majority of instances, this is put off until it is far too late. Fish are seldom in good condition after the middle of August. The ova begins to become large, and the fish is not in good order for the table; and therefore, if some period towards the middle of August were fixed on for its commencement, the rivers and the public would derive very great benefit from it.

But it is needless to say that the close-time should be rigidly kept and enforced, and any one found destroying or molesting the fish during that period should be most severely punished. At present, however, such is the reckless disregard to it, that during the last close-season, no less than 100 tons of fish—most of them in a spawning and all in a foul and unwholesome state—were exported to France alone. The fish are then unfit for food, and therefore the sacrifice of this unwholesome food, the exportation of which is so destructive to our fisheries, is not a very great one to ask. I believe that there are some hopes, owing to the exertions of the society above named, that this exportation will be prohibited.

The other matters detrimental to salmon are mine and mill refuse. These have been dealt with mildly in the English Act, to which I refer the reader for regulations as regards weirs and fry-killing, &c., which upon the whole are reasonably good, save that netting should not be allowed to be carried on in the immediate proximity of fish-passes, or fish-passes will be rendered useless.

II.

THE STOCKING OF THE CLYDE WITH GREYLING.

In 1858, Mr. J. J. Briggs sent the account of which the accompanying extract is a small part to the *Field*. He is quoting from Mr. Eyre's Journal, kept to note down any facts that might be interesting. The Clyde is now thoroughly stocked with greyling, which are even of finer size than the trout which are found in it. Three or four dozen a day is an ordinary day's sport :—

"Mr. Eyre says :—

"'On the 13th of April, 1857, the temperature of the air being 40° Fahr., we netted about 200 greyling near Bakewell, and expressed the spawn and milt from about fifty of them. Of the rest some had spawned, and many were too young. The spawn was put into common wine-bottles, about half-filled with water, and sent off the same night to Abington, on the Clyde, about fifty miles above Glasgow. The West of Scotland Angling Club had already prepared a rill for its reception. About 10,000 ova were sent, and I retained some hundreds for experiments. They were about one-eighth of an inch in diameter. The following remarks are extracted from my diary, the progress of the greyling from the ovum state to that of the perfect fish being observed daily with a microscope :—

"'*4th day.*—They seem a little larger, and consist of an outer vesicle of elastic membrane, filled with a semi-transparent fluid, and of an inner vesicle or yolk filled with a yellow granular substance, and on the inner vesicle is a spot indicating the germ of the future fish.

"'*6th day.*—The form is slightly altered. The fluid appears flocculent.

"'*8th day.*—The live fœtus is visible. It is of a semi-transparent yellow-amber colour; the head in three lobes. The fish lashes its tail violently at regular intervals, eight or ten times a minute. The granules partially absorbed.

"'*10th day.*—Temperature of the room, 55°; river (Derwent), 52°. Fœtus less active.

"'*30th day.*—The fœtus made its first partial detachment from the enveloping membrane by freeing its tail. About half-an-hour afterwards it entirely and suddenly disconnected itself from the chorion, which sank to the bottom of the glass. Temperature, 60°. The eyes well developed, the mouth seems still closed. The umbilical sac filled with granular matter attached to the thorax. Pulsation regular. Above the place of the hinder part of the gill-cover a constant and rapid motion is apparent, above 160 per minute. This may be from the vibrating edge of a fine membrane, which at present forms a substitute for the true gills, or it may be from the rapid circulation of the blood in loops coming to the water to be ærated, or it may be from cilia on the edge of the membrane. The membrane, or whatever looks like it, is so transparent that it is difficult to decide. The markings of the vertebræ are apparent. The place of the vent is indicated by a scarlet spot.

" '33*rd day*.—The mouth is now in constant but slow motion ; the yolk-sac much lessened in size.

" '41*st day*.—The young fish are now perfect, and are about nine-tenths of an inch in length, and the umbilical sac is absorbed.

" 'These ova were daily examined by being placed under the microscope or other magnifier, and part continually destroyed, probably from the concentrated light of the lenses. On one occasion Mr. Eyre and Mr. Peach were examining a rather forward-looking ovum *under the microscope*, when the fish, by an instantaneous effort, burst the membrane or *chorion*, and in a few minutes after they saw him, by another effort, free himself entirely from it. This was a piece of wonderful good fortune, as that particular operation might have been watched for for years fruitlessly.

" 'In the natural rill falling into the Clyde, the *first fish* appeared on *the seventeenth* day, and the average was twenty days. In some ova placed in boxes through which the same rill ran, the average time was forty days.

" 'In June, 1857, these fish were about the size of minnows, healthy, and in the evening rose freely at small flies. I estimated their number at 3,000 or 4,000.

" 'In March 1858 they were on the average five inches in length (some reached 6¼), and were doing well.' "

III.

STORMONTFIELD.

THE experiments, or rather operations, in the breeding of young salmon at Stormontfield, on the Tay, were commenced in 1853, at the instance of Dr. Esdaile and Mr. Ashworth. A gentle slope from a mill-lade, running parallel with and sixteen feet above the Tay, was chosen, whence a sufficient supply of water could be obtained. Three hundred boxes were laid down in twenty-five parallel rows, each box being partly filled with clean gravel and pebbles, and protected at each end by perforated zinc. Filtering-beds were formed at the head and foot of the rows, and the boxes were charged with 300,000 ova by the 23rd of December.

On the 31st of March, 1854, the first ova were hatched. A pond had been provided for the fry; this pond was 223 feet long, by 112 feet in the broadest part. It was subsequently found to be far too small. By June the greater part of the fry were admitted into the pond, being then about an inch and a half long. There they were fed with boiled liver daily, and on the 24th of May, or nearly twelve months after their being hatched, a large portion of them, having assumed the smolt scale, left the pond

and commenced their descent to the sea; an equally
large number remaining behind, and showing no dis-
position to assume the migratory dress of the smolt.
Many of the smolts which then migrated were marked
by the cutting off of the adipose fin,[1] *and a large number
of them were retaken, ascending the river again, at various
periods up to August, in the form of grilse,* and varying in
weight from 6lbs. to 9lbs., according to the time they had
remained in the salt-water—thus distinctly proving the
disputed question as to the rate of growth of salmon.
It was thought that the singular case of some fry remaining in the river for two or three, and others only for
one year, might be the result of some carelessness in
conducting the experiment, by using grilse and salmon
indiscriminately; but subsequent attempts have shown
that it was not so, as during the last season the spawn
was taken only from the best and healthiest full-grown
salmon, no grilse being used; and the result has been
precisely the same as formerly — so that this curious
problem in the natural history of the salmon still remains
to be solved.

From 1853 to 1862, the boxes were stocked five several
times. One of these, that of 1854, proved a failure. It
was found impossible to stock the boxes oftener than
every other year, owing to the limited accommodation for
the fry. Great benefits must have accrued to the Tay

[1] Many plans of a different kind were tried subsequently for
marking the smolts by rings, wires, &c.; but none of them were
found to answer, save the cutting off of the adipose or small soft
fin which is peculiar to the Salmonidæ.

from these operations, but it was rendered impossible to estimate them, by reason of the prejudice and ignorance of the fishermen, who failed to send notice to Mr. Buist of the marked fish recaptured, so that the proportion of fry that returned to the river as grilse and salmon could not be computed. Thus, one of the most valuable statistical results of the experiments was altogether lost, a fact very much to be regretted. Many most interesting and hitherto debatable points in the natural history of the salmon were also cleared up in the course of the experiments, and science owes a debt of gratitude to the conductors of them. To those who desire a compendious and circumstantial history of these operations, I recommend strongly Mr. Brown's little work upon the Stormontfield Experiments, which is a valuable contribution to the natural history of the salmon.

IV.

MR. ASHWORTH'S UNDERTAKINGS.

SEVERAL successful undertakings in pisciculture have been
carried out in Ireland. The first of any note, perhaps,
was at Outerard, near Galway, in 1852. The Galway
River is the channel through which Loughs Mask and
Corrib, two enormous lakes containing a vast area of
water, discharge themselves into the sea. The fishery of
this river belongs to Mr. Ashworth. In 1852, finding the
stock had been terribly reduced from a variety of causes,
he established a breeding-place at Outerard, in a small
tributary stream. Here twenty boxes were laid down, after
the same fashion as the plan, already explained, adopted
at Stormontfield. This plan, carried out by Mr. Ramsbottom, was the model whence Stormontfield was taken.
These boxes were stocked with about 40,000 ova, which
in due time came to perfection. Subsequently, owing
partly to the opening of a wide Queen's-gap in the weir,
Mr. Ashworth's fishery multiplied itself in value many-
fold, and he cast about, adding a still larger area to the
field of his operations.

Lough Mask, which discharges into Lough Corrib,
is separated from it by a very rugged channel and

a lofty, impassable fall; consequently, although Lough Corrib abounded in salmon, none had ever been seen in Lough Mask. Moreover, the many gravelly tributaries which salmon love to spawn in rather discharged themselves into the upper part of Lough Mask, which again receives the waters of one or two smaller lakes than Lough Corrib; and as the capabilities of production of a fishery are bounded by the area of its spawning-beds, this proved a serious check to the further increase of productiveness in the fishery. Undaunted by difficulties, however, Mr. Ashworth set to work, ameliorated the stream, put salmon-stairs to the impassable fall, and stocked the head waters of Lough Mask with half-a-million of salmon ova. These operations have been so lately completed, that we hardly know as yet what measure of success will attend them; but I see no reason for doubting their success, and if so, a capable area of about thirty square miles will be added to Mr. Ashworth's already valuable fishery, and in a few years' time the fishery will realize a handsome fortune. This shows what can be done by pisciculture, in its broad sense, and a little practical common sense combined.

V.

MR. COOPER'S EXPERIMENT AT BALLISODARE.

THIS undertaking, which was really an experiment, shows
how great difficulties can be overcome by perseverance, and
how a fishery can be created where none has previously
existed.   Mr. Cooper owns two rivers, the Owenmore and
the Arrow, which unite some two-and-a-half miles from
the sea and form the Ballisodare River.   On these rivers
are three falls : the lowest, which is a succession of falls
over high ledges of rock, is within a short distance of
the sea ; the next, which is a short distance above it, is
called the Upper Ballisodare Fall.   This fall is impracticable to fish, though fish had been known to surmount
the lower one occasionally, but not often.   The entire
height of the two falls is about seventy feet.   The highest,
which is on the Owenmore, near the village of Collooney,
has but one fall ; but this one is higher than either of the
falls which comprise the lower one and the Upper Ballisodare Fall, and is entirely impracticable.

The ladder applied to the Upper Ballisodare Fall was
at first brought out into the lower water too far down the
stream from the fall, so that the fish in running up missed

it. It was therefore found necessary to turn it, so as to bring the embouchure of the ladder close to the foot of the falls. A few pairs of fish had always been in the habit of entering the river and running up to the lower falls, and the plan adopted to stock the river was that of catching the fish and placing them in the river above the falls, so that they might spawn in the river. After sundry failures, the ladders being completed and several fish being put up above the falls, and a small portion of ova deposited in the river, a large quantity of salmon-fry was observed to be in the river. These, at the usual time, became smolts and disappeared. This was about April, 1857. On June 26th the first grilse was observed at the fall; by July they were plentiful, and so continued till the end of the season. The river was not fished in 1857.

I had much more and interesting particulars from Mr. Cooper in reference to this fishery, but cannot find space for it here. The account was fully given in the *Field* in December, 1858, and from that paper I extract the following table, showing how completely the experiment succeeded. The table was kept by an agent whom Mr. Cooper appointed :—

" ' 1857. August 24. Saw several salmon in the hole under the fall of Collooney.

" ' September 24. The river between Ballisodare and Collooney is now well stocked, salmon being visible in almost every deep hole, and a number being congregated between Collooney Bridge and the hole under the fall.

" ' October 3. A flood being in the Owenmore, I shut the water off the Collooney ladder to see if there were any fish passing up, and found seven salmon and one white trout in the pond. Of these seven, five were males.

"'October 13. Examined Collooney ladder, and reported to Mr. Leech that there were salmon in it. Twenty-seven salmon were found in it, the great majority of them being females.

"'October 15. Lowered the sluice of Collooney ladder again, but got no fish.

"'October 28. Again examined the ladder, and got three male fish.

"'October 30. Four male and two female fish taken out of ladder and put up.

"'November 3. Sixteen male and eight female.

"'November 4. There were ten fish in the ladder, which were not removed, as Mr. Leech was not present.

"'November 5. Nine fish, not removed.

"'November 6. Seven ditto, ditto.

"'November 7. Eleven ditto, ditto. I went to Ballisodare on this day, and saw several large fish leaping at the upper ladder.

"'November 9. We put up from the ladder twenty-four male and fifteen female fish.

"'November 23. Lowered the sluice again ; twenty-five male and twenty female fish found in the pond. A few of these were large fish, say 14lbs. or 15lbs. weight.

"'November 30. The fish are now beginning to spawn in great numbers in the Owenbeg River.

"'December 3. Thirty-six male and forty-five female fish found in the ladder.

"'1858. January 5. Saw a few spawning-beds in Owenmore.

"'January 9. In River Arrow and tributaries found twenty-nine salmon redds.

"'February 14. Walked the Kilmorgan River (a tributary to the Arrow), and counted twenty-one redds.'

"In the early part of this year, 1858, we seldom fished. In the month of February we took five fish; in March three; in April two: in May ten; in June thirty-nine. We did not, in fact, begin to fish regularly till the 1st July. During this month we took 868 salmon, and up to the 20th August (the close of our season) 530 more—the year's take averaging very little more than 4lbs. each. Mr. Culbertson's notes on this year are: 'Spring-fish showing in February. One of 9lbs., taken in the net, was a fry marked by Brown in 1856. In March got another about the same weight. Only a few fish through this month. Fry coming down in April, and more plentiful in May: but I do not think so many in the river as last year. On 13th May saw nearly one hundred jumps from six to eight o'clock in the evening; they were from 8lbs. to 12lbs. weight. On 9th June saw first grilse at lower fall; about the end of the month they were very plentiful. Among the fish taken by the nets on 6th July, seven were fry marked by me last year, and they weighed 5½lbs. to 6lbs. each.'

"Since the end of the close-season, many reports have been sent me relative to the numbers running up. From my inspector's book I take the following: 'Aug. 28. At Ballisodare numbers of salmon in every part of the river between bridge and lowest fall. Sept. 1. Collooney ladder literally full of fish. They did not run in such numbers last year until November, being over two months earlier this year. Sept. 6. Plenty of fish immediately above Collooney Bridge. Sept. 25. Collooney ladder swarming, and plenty showing in every place between bridge and fall. October 3 to 6. Heavy floods. Collooney ladder resembles a steeplechase, as we see them clearing the steps in pairs, and some very good fish. Oct. 8 and 9. Plenty of fish still on the run. Oct. 16. I have been watching the salmon jumping and playing at Collooney fall and ladder. I have visited the ladder daily this week, and from the numbers in it, am convinced that they could be removed from top of ladder with the hand. Nov. 27. Great numbers of fish in Collooney ladder.' In addition to these notes of my inspector, one of my water-keepers reported having counted 267 salmon in one hour ascending the Collooney ladder ; and Mr. Culbertson has written to me to say that he reckoned 100 in less than half-an-hour making up the the rapids at Ballisodare. On yesterday, Dec. 2, there were so many fish in the pond at Collooney, that Mr. Leech took up no less than six at once in a common landing-net.

" EDWARD J. COOPER.

Markree Castle, December 3.

" P. S.—Since my letter was written, the Earl of Enniskillen has visited my fishery ; and I extract the following from his notes, entered in inspector's book :—

" ' On the 9th (Dec.) I visited Collooney ladder, and saw immense quantities of fish running up. Frequently saw four fish at the upper step jumping together. On the 10th again at Collooney. Not nearly so many fish moving this day; counted at upper step nineteen in five minutes. Turned off the water, and put up 256 fish. This day (11th) counted 102 fish jump at the upper step in five minutes. Turned off the water; the pond actually alive with fish, in general larger and fresher from the sea than those of yesterday. Put up 246 fish, and then stopped as the fish were getting sick in the pond. I am confident that we did not take half the number out, and that we left from three to four hundred in the pond.' "

VI.

SALMON STAIRS.

I HAVE spoken of salmon-stairs. These are certain ap
pliances adapted to falls or weirs, for the purpose of
breaking one large fall into a number of small ones, and
so giving the ascending fish an opportunity of breaking

the journey up it. When the fall is tolerably light and not
perpendicular, as over weirs for example, the task is easy.
A large trough is fitted to the weir, the part being selected

where most water flows over. In this trough are fixed stout, transverse boards or steps, properly supported, to resist the weight of the stream. Stone will be found cheapest in the long run. These boards do not of course continue entirely across the trough, so as to bar the fish out; but an opening is left at either side alternately, through which the fish *can rush*.

The accompanying diagram will illustrate the manner in which this is contrived. The arrows denote the direction of the stream, and it will be seen that behind every step the salmon can find a safe resting-place. When the fall is very heavy and perpendicular, it is less expensive to make a cut round it, which is done by digging a passage from some distance above it, as close to the foot of the fall as possible,—this cut, of course, being broken up by steps into a series of small falls, easily practicable to the fish. This plan was adopted at Ballisodare and at Lough Mask.

VII.

COREGONUS LAVARETUS AND FERA.

I GIVE here short descriptions by Dr. Carl Voght of the above two fish; not of course adopting those descriptions or opinions, but simply that students may have an opportunity of weighing testimony :—

" THE GANGFISH.

"The Lavaret (*Coregonus Lavaretus* or *Wartmanni*) of the Lakes of Bourget, Geneva, and Neuenberg, appears to be the same variety as the *Palée blanche* of the Neuburg Lake, the *Neuerling, Stuben, Gangfisch, Renker Drewer,* the *Blanfölchen* of the Lake of Constance, the *Balchen* of the Lakes of Zug and Lucerne, the *Aalbock* of the Thun and Brienz Lakes, the *Edelfish* of the Lake of Lucerne, and the *Renke* of the Upper Bavarian lakes.

" BODEN-RENKE (*Coregonus Fera*).

"A second larger species of the Fera (*Coregonus Fera*) of the Lake of Geneva, the *Weisfölchen* or *Sand-gangfish* of the Lake of Constance, the *Bläuling* or *Bratfish* of the Lake of Zurich, the *Boden-renke* of the Starnberg Lake."

In acclimatizing this fish, the French do not send the ova from Huningue with the embryo developed, as they do all the other ova, because the eggs are so small as to render manipulation difficult. They, therefore, send them out as quickly as possible after they are taken, and request that they may be immediately distributed. They advise them to be sown, like grain (thrown broadcast as it were), in the shallow shores of lakes and ponds. If hatched in confinement, they should be placed on a bed of weeds partially submerged : they need not be plunged in the water themselves. When hatched, the young do not remain helpless at the bottom for five or six weeks, like the other Salmonidæ, but swim at once on the top : they should then be immediately set at liberty. If kept in confinement, their food (liver) should be ground to dust and cast upon the surface of the water. Such are the directions sent forth in respect to the Fera.

Of course, where varieties caused by waters and locality are as plentiful as the lakes ; where the distinctive differences between the fish themselves are but small, and where names are legion, as in the above description, the confusion is so great that nothing but the utmost patience and perseverance, combined with large opportunities and the staunchest assistance, can ever hope to settle such moot points as these questions of the identity of some fish with others. The Coregoni are, therefore, as yet very much unexplored and debatable ground with naturalists.

THE END.

www.ingramcontent.com/pod-product-compliance
Lightning Source LLC
Chambersburg PA
CBHW030338270326
41926CB00009B/879